···☽ THE ZENNED OUT GUIDE TO ☾···

UNDERSTANDING
TAROT

YOUR HANDBOOK TO READING
AND INTUITING THE TAROT

First published in 2021 by Rock Point,
an imprint of The Quarto Group,
142 West 36th Street, 4th Floor,
New York, NY 10018, USA
T (212) 779-4972 F (212) 779-6058
www.QuartoKnows.com

Rock Point titles are also available at discount for retail, wholesale, promotional, and bulk purchase. For details, contact the Special Sales Manager by email at specialsales@quarto.com or by mail at The Quarto Group, Attn: Special Sales Manager, 100 Cummings Center Suite 265D, Beverly, MA 01915 USA.

10 9 8 7 6 5 4 3 2 1

ISBN: 978-1-63106-773-0

Library of Congress Control Number: 2021938206

PUBLISHER: Rage Kindelsperger
CREATIVE DIRECTOR: Laura Drew
MANAGING EDITOR: Cara Donaldson
EDITOR: Keyla Pizarro-Hernández
COVER AND INTERIOR DESIGN: Sydney Martenis

Printed in China

THE ZENNED OUT GUIDE TO

UNDERSTANDING TAROT

YOUR HANDBOOK TO READING AND INTUITING THE TAROT

CASSIE UHL

ROCK
POINT

⸱⸱⸱✦ INTRODUCTION ✦⸱⸱⸱

The tarot is one of the most beloved treasures among mystics, psychics, and intuitives. In fact, I'd argue that it's the most common divination tool that we see used today. It's risen above the ranks of palmistry, tea leaf reading, crystal ball gazing, and scrying.

How is it that a simple deck of cards has made such an impression on us? I believe it's because the tarot tells us a story, a story about ourselves. The tarot uncovers our greatest strengths and our deepest secrets. It reveals our weaknesses and our innermost desires.

The tarot acts as a mirror to our soul, reflecting back to us precisely what we need to continue growing into the best versions of ourselves. We can gain divine wisdom about ourselves and our lives by merely understanding the stories within the tarot.

THE TAROT ACTS AS A POTENT
SELF-DISCOVERY SYSTEM THAT HAS THE
POWER TO CATAPULT YOU INTO THE
FARTHEST REACHES OF YOUR SOUL.

In this book, you'll gain all of the necessary tools to understand and interpret the messages and stories within the 78 cards of the tarot. We'll explore tarot through the lens of the four elements (earth, air, water, and fire), numerology, and astrology. I'll also share common tarot vocabulary, how to select a deck, how to perform readings, and, of course, a handy card-meaning glossary.

As the founder of the spirituality brand, Zenned Out, artist, writer, and someone who's worked with tarot cards for a multitude of magickal uses for years, I have a unique perspective to share with you. I do not just work with the tarot for divination, but also use them for spellwork, shadow work, energy readings, and more. The card meanings I offer in this book are based off of the deep relationships I formed with the cards, which I believe you'll be able to sense and experience as you explore this book.

If this is your first step into the world of tarot, I'm so excited for you to embark on this life-changing journey. If tarot is already a trusted companion, I trust that this book will spark a renewed sense of wonder in your relationship with the deck.

⋯☆ HOW TO USE THIS BOOK ☆⋯

First, I want you to know that you don't have to be a psychic to work with the tarot. What you will need is a tarot card deck of your choosing. It's okay if you don't have one yet, but it will certainly help you put this book to better use!

> ⋅•◌ TIP ◌•⋅
>
> **Working with the tarot will undoubtedly improve your intuitive abilities, but proficiency is not a prerequisite!**

The deck used throughout this book is my tarot card deck, *The Zenned Out Journey Tarot*. Of course, I think my deck is a great option, but any deck will do! *The Zenned Out Journey Tarot* deck is based on the most common tarot deck, the Rider-Waite-Smith, so you'll see that all of the cards' names have remained the same for easy use with this deck and most other decks. If you need help selecting a deck, I'll cover pointers in the next chapter.

The first four chapters of this book contain all of the foundational information about working with the tarot. Read it in any order that you like, but I suggest reading it all, as it will help you use the tarot to its full potential. The glossary of card meanings in later chapters can be read in order, but it's not necessary.

Personally, I've found the best way to learn the cards is to start working with them ASAP. It's easy to get stuck in a mind-set that you have to memorize all of the cards before you start working with them. Feel free to read the glossary of card descriptions if you feel called, and reference it as often as you like, but don't let it be the Achilles' heel that prevents you from actually working with the cards. You might also find it helpful to start a tarot journal—nothing fancy, just a place to write down how the cards speak to you and make notes about your card readings.

⋯⭐ TRUSTING YOUR JOURNEY ⭐⋯

When I purchased my first tarot deck as a teenager, my mom quickly warned me of its "evils" and expressed to me that it was "ungodly" to try to tell the future. This really discouraged me at first. It also confused me, but that was because I didn't fully understand the tarot's power at that young age.

Fortunately, as I grew older, I came back to the tarot. I did my own research and worked with the 78 cards in my personal practice. I discovered that not only was there nothing evil about tarot but also that it was designed as a self-discovery tool to help us reach our fullest potential. Can it be used as a divination tool? Yes, of course (which, in my opinion, is not "ungodly" in the slightest). My years of working with the tarot taught me that its most valuable asset is its ability to show you what you need to flourish into the highest and best version of yourself.

I tell you this to remind you to always trust your journey. If the tarot has come into your life, or you feel drawn to it, trust that. Don't let anyone discourage you from working with this tool. There's a reason the tarot has stood the test of time. The tarot is a powerful healing tool, and its truest aim is to help you become a better human.

INTUITION IS THE
VOICE OF THE SOUL.
TRUST IT.

CHAPTER 1

GETTING STARTED WITH THE TAROT

The most important thing I can teach you about working with the tarot is that your journey will be uniquely yours. The twists and turns the tarot has taken to get to where it is today (which I'll touch on later in this chapter) says a lot about what working with the tarot feels like on a personal level. Working with the tarot is a nonlinear process, and there are many ways to approach the enlightening practice held within these 78 cards.

What I offer you here are the building blocks to form a tarot practice that works for and makes sense to you. I share what has worked for me but want to preface it with an understanding that it is not the only way. Though tarot may not be as ancient as some believe, it is an extremely rich and varied practice. Many roads can lead to the same destination.

For example, in my practice, I primarily focus on the four elements (earth, air, water, and fire), numerology, and astrology for working with the tarot. There are many who use Jewish mysticism and Kabbalah as a frame of reference for the tarot. Working with the tarot in this way is just as valid as the way I work with the tarot, but because I'm not Jewish, I don't include it in my practice. That said, if you have roots in Judaism, I encourage you to continue to expand your tarot knowledge with teachers who reflect your heritage. This goes for any spiritual practice!

The building blocks I provide in this chapter will help you get to know the tarot. I'll share what you can expect to gain from working with the tarot, a brief history of the tarot, and how to select a deck. I'll also dissect the term *fortune telling* and teach you a few ways to start pulling cards.

WHY WORK WITH TAROT CARDS?

♦ The tarot offers you deep insight into the way you move through the world.

♦ It is a perfect tool for honing your intuition.

♦ You'll learn the positive and negative aspects of the most common archetypes and better understand how they relate to you and your loved ones.

♦ It helps you make decisions, big and small.

♦ The tarot acts as a mirror to your soul and subconscious.

♦ You'll become familiar with a variety of other energetic correspondences used throughout the tarot, like the four elements, numerology, and astrology.

♦ The tarot can also be used to gain clarity on your path ahead and future events.

⋯✯ A BRIEF HISTORY OF TAROT ✯⋯

You might be wondering where this marvelous and mysterious deck of cards came from. The history of the tarot is quite enthralling and could quite easily fill this entire book! There are many different perspectives about the origins of the tarot. If you're into history, I encourage you to dive deeper on your own, but for now, I'll give you the highlights.

There are a few different pathways when it comes to where the tarot originated. Some choose to only look at the facts that are clearly documented; others choose to read between the lines and make inferences about connections between tarot and more ancient civilizations. Personally, I believe there's truth in both. I'll let you decide for yourself.

The earliest cards that resemble the numbered cards in the tarot are known as the Mamluk deck from thirteenth-century Egypt. The Mamluk deck was likely inspired by paper card games from China. In the early Mamluk decks, we see four suites of Polo Sticks, Swords, Cups, and Coins, which are very similar to the Wands, Cups, Swords, Coins (Pentacles) of today's modern tarot. What you don't see in these early decks are the detailed stories told on the trump cards of the Major Arcana.

We may never know the true origins of the tarot, but what we do know is that it has served as a powerful tool to shed light on our human journey for centuries. The earliest origins of tarot card decks with the 21 trump cards (that we have documented proof of) appear in Northern Italy in the early fifteenth century. These early decks were initially created as nothing more than a game, similar to bridge. But don't let this stop you from believing in the magic of tarot!

The mystical history of the tarot takes a lot of twists and turns at this point. Some of the big players in the development of the mystical and divinatory version of the tarot are Court de Gebelin, Eteilla, Eliphas Levi, the Hermetic Order of the Golden Dawn, and eventually Arthur Edward Waite and Pamela Coleman Smith. Now, this is a huge oversimplification (like I said, please dig deeper if this sparks your interest!), but the people and group listed above started to draw connections between the story of the tarot cards and all sorts of deeper meaning, occult symbolism, and ancient wisdom.

Just because, according to history, the tarot didn't originate deep in a mystical cave by ancient Atlantean priests and priestesses doesn't mean that it hasn't been molded into a powerful healing tool. If you want more proof, I think you'll be swayed in the coming pages and in your individual work with the tarot. But don't take my word for it—try it for yourself!

HOW DOES THE TAROT WORK AND IS IT FORTUNE TELLING?

The term *fortune telling* has done a disservice to the healing power of tarot because the tarot offers *so* much more than telling the future. Now, this is another one that you can find a lot of different opinions on, but personally, I view the tarot as a window to the soul, subconscious, and higher self. The tarot is a spiritual learning tool that has the power to offer you wisdom and insight into your life, but only when you're ready to receive it.

I get that what you really want to know is whether you can tell the future with tarot cards. The answer is yes, but psychics have been telling the future with tea leaves, palms, crystal balls, their minds, and more since the beginning of time. Predicting the future is something humans have been doing forever. This has more to do with your intuition, which is a big part of tarot, but not the only part. The tarot invites you on a journey into your soul through story and symbols.

The tarot offers a look at your soul at this moment. The archetypes, symbols, and layered meanings of each card in the tarot shine a light on your deepest desires and subconscious mind. Talk about powerful! Of course, a skilled tarot reader can also shine the light of truth on people they're reading for, but we'll discuss that more in a future chapter!

THE STRUCTURE OF
THE TAROT DECK

The tarot deck begins with the 22 Major Arcana. These are the heavy hitters of the tarot. They start the deck with the Fool at "0" and end with The World, the Major Arcana at card 22. These cards are often the most detailed cards of the deck because they have the biggest stories to tell, both individually and as a collection. The Major Arcana work together to tell a story, often called The Fool's Journey or The Hero's Journey. It's for this reason that the Fool is usually depicted as being 0. This card is a separate energy from the story of the Major Arcana. These cards often present as big life themes in readings. They're not cards you want to ignore when you pull one!

The Major Arcana can be divided into three lines, which makes seeing and understanding the story it tells clearer. The Fool is left out of the three lines, and the rest of the cards are divided into three equal rows of seven. See the guide on page 20 for reference. Each line of the Major Arcana tells a story of its own as you move closer to the enlightenment and attainment associated with judgment and the world—of course, only to begin the journey again.

The 56 Minor Arcana follow the Majors and consist of four suits divided into 14 cards each. The four suits are Cups, Swords, Wands, and Pentacles or Coins. Each suit has 10 numbered cards, also called "pip cards," and 4 court cards: Pages, Knights, Queens, and Kings. The Minor Arcana offers messages about everyday life. They're important, but not to the same magnitude as the Major Arcana. Court cards signal important people in your life (Pages usually represent children, Knights represent teens, Queens represent mother figures, and Kings represent father figures).

Each suit of the Minor Arcana tells a story too and corresponds to one of the four elements. We'll dive into this more deeply in the next chapter.

For the most part, this information will stay true for any tarot card pack you buy. However, it's common to find newer card decks with the names of the Major Arcana changed and some of the suites altered as well. Even with these more modern interpretations, the meanings of the cards remain rather consistent.

Now that you understand the history and basics of tarot, let's get you a deck and learn how to select cards.

THE THREE LINES OF
THE MAJOR ARCANA

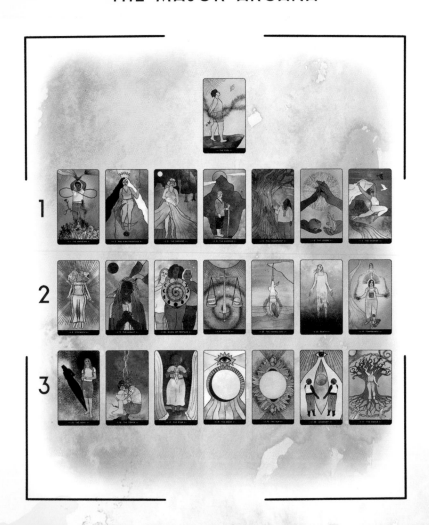

⋯✦ COMMON TAROT TERMS ✦⋯

MAJOR ARCANA
The first 22 cards of the tarot depicting "The Fool's Journey."

MINOR ARCANA
The 56 cards that follow the Major Arcana; these are divided into four suits.

TAROT SUITS
The four suits of the Minor Arcana: Wands, Cups, Swords, and Pentacles or Coins.

PIP CARDS
The numbered cards in the Minor Arcana.

TRUMP CARDS
Another name for the Major Arcana.

COURT CARDS
The Pages, Knights, Queens, and Kings of the Minor Arcana.

⋯✮ HOW TO SELECT A DECK ✮⋯

The simple answer to selecting your perfect tarot deck is to choose something that you resonate with, but I know that's easier said than done with the number of options available. Let's weigh some of the pros and cons of the most common choices.

The most common deck is the Rider-Waite-Smith deck by A. E. Waite and artist Pamela Coleman Smith. If you know anything about tarot, you've probably seen images of cards from this deck. It's not only the most common deck, but it's also the most common deck that other artists reference when creating their own deck (myself included!). This deck is a great starter deck because most tarot card books and meanings reference it. That said, there are many things about this deck that turn people off, like the religious connotations and the fact that the imagery is outdated.

Fortunately, there are oodles of artists who've created modernized versions of the treasured Rider-Waite-Smith deck. Some of them have kept all of the same names of the Major Arcana and Minor Arcana, and some have updated them. When deciding on a tarot deck, it is helpful to determine whether you want to get a deck that has used the same names for the trump cards and suits as the Rider-Waite-Smith deck or whether you want a deck with different names. Most books and online sources offer card descriptions for the traditional Rider-Waite-Smith deck, so if your deck has modified names, you may experience more difficulty finding alternative card descriptions.

Don't let the card descriptions stop you from buying a deck that catches your eye. This is where your intuition comes in and is part of the magic of the tarot. There are many who believe that you should throw out the guidebook and rely solely on your intuition when interpreting the cards. This can certainly be a powerful method, but it will require you to hone and refine your intuition.

Like most things in life, I find a good balance between intuition and learning the deeper meanings of the cards to be a wonderful option. I suggest starting with the basics when learning the card meanings, which I'll outline in the coming chapters, so you have a solid foundation for your intuition to take off.

·•◊ TIP ◊•·

When choosing a tarot card deck, try these three tips to see if it's a good fit. Hold the deck in your hand, and notice how it makes you feel. Look at the images of the cards, do they spark your curiosity or make you feel lit up inside? Look at the names assigned to the cards in the Major Arcana, do they make you feel safe and supported? If you answer "yes!" to these questions, it might be your deck!

CHAPTER 2

TAROT CORRESPONDENCES

C orrespondence is a fancy word that means energies that match, or as I like to say, "play nicely together." Learning the fundamental correspondences for the different tarot cards will help you learn the card meanings much faster. It will also help you understand the cards on a deeper level and help you connect them with each other to start to build stories within the tarot.

In this chapter, you'll learn the basics of the four elements, numerology, and astrology. Each of these studies is woven throughout the tarot and corresponds with different tarot cards. If you find you resonate with any of these topics, I encourage you to explore them even more, as you'll undoubtedly be able to apply them to your tarot knowledge as well. If you're already familiar with some of the topics I cover in this chapter, then you'll be that much faster at applying your knowledge to the tarot! The nice thing about learning tarot correspondences is that you'll likely find ways to apply them to other parts of your spiritual or witchy practices.

·○◊ TIP ◁○·

There are far more correspondences in the tarot besides the elements, numerology, and astrology (but I do believe these are the best starting place!). If you feel called to learn other tarot correspondences, I suggest learning more about common archetypes, colors, symbolism, and Hebrew letters.

✦ THE FOUR ELEMENTS ✦

The four elements are four universal qualities present all around and within you. They are essential to all life. You and the Universe are formed by these four elements: earth, air, water, and fire. The elements go far beyond the physical and also manifest as personality traits and energetic forces.

EACH ELEMENT CARRIES ITS OWN SET OF QUALITIES. NO ELEMENT IS INHERENTLY BAD OR GOOD. THEY EACH CARRY AN EQUAL AMOUNT OF POSITIVE AND NEGATIVE TRAITS.

The elements are here to bring balance, both physically and energetically. In nature, fire needs water to be quenched, and the earth needs air to move and grow. The elements are reflected in your personality as well. For example, you might consider yourself very fiery or have a lot of fire in your astrological birth chart (that's a topic for another day!), and this plays a role in how you express yourself. The elements of your personality can be balanced just like nature. If you're a very fiery person and need to balance it out, you can add slower and softer routines associated with the element of water, like taking a bath.

How does all of this play into the tarot? Each suit of the Minor Arcana is represented by one of the four elements and invites you on a journey to deeply explore each element. The heavy hitters of tarot—the Major Arcana—aren't left out of this either. Each of the Major Arcana cards corresponds to one of the elements, which offers you another way to understand and interact with these cards as well. Let's dive a little deeper into each of the elements.

·◦◌ TIP ◌◦·

As you explore the four elements in the tarot, I encourage you to become more aware of the elements in nature. Ask yourself: "How does each element show up in nature?" and "What purpose does each element serve in the natural world?" Noticing the elements in your environment will help give you clues to how they show up in the tarot.

UNDERSTANDING THE ENERGY
OF THE FOUR ELEMENTS

AIR
Communication, ideas,
inspiration, learning, spirituality

EARTH
Comfort, physicality, grounding,
safety, materiality

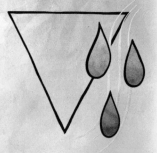

FIRE
Energy, authority, action,
anger, strength

WATER
Emotions, healing, creativity,
adaptability, sensuality

THE ELEMENTS IN THE MINOR ARCANA

SWORDS
Air

PENTACLES
Earth

WANDS
Fire

CUPS
Water

WATER

In the tarot, the element of water is easy to spot in the Suit of Cups. Cups, vessels, and chalices have all been associated with feminine energy and creation. The element of water is the seat of emotions and is ruled by the moon. Water is a feminine and flowing energy but can also be incredibly powerful. Think about water in nature. It can be a still pond, a powerful waterfall, or a solid iceberg. Even though this is often considered a softer energy, it has the power to bring you to your knees, both physically and through your emotions!

On an energetic level, water asks you to allow your emotions, all of them. This element does not see good or bad emotions. It just asks you to feel them so you can process them. When the element of water is balanced in a person, they will allow their emotions to flow freely, processing them as they come up. When someone bottles up their emotions, we can see the powerful nature of water with explosive emotional reactions.

ALLOW THE DEPTHS OF YOUR EMOTIONS
TO FLOW. YOUR INTERNAL OCEANS HOLD
DEEP WISDOM.

Creativity and sensuality are also strong themes of the element of water. We can see this in the correspondence to the sacral chakra and womb space. Sensuality and sexuality are both modes of creativity and lead to the creation of life itself. When our sexual nature is repressed, we can see the element of water surface as stifled creativity and a leaning toward more masculine characteristics. When in a state of flow with water, creative energy will move through you with ease.

Water can take many forms: liquid, solid, and vapor. Your emotions are similar, changing and flowing. Mastering the element of water means you're able to allow these transformations and changes within you, so they manifest in healthy ways, even if what's coming up feels hard or scary. We can see the power of water in nature, and it is not an element you want to hold back.

···☆ WATER CORRESPONDENCES ☆···

·•◊ TAROT MINOR ARCANA ◊•·
Suit of Cups and the Queens

·•◊ TAROT MAJOR ARCANA ◊•·
High Priestess, Moon, Hanged One, Chariot, Death

·•◊ BODY ◊•·
The womb space

·•◊ CHAKRA ◊•·
Sacral

·•◊ PLANETS ◊•·
The Moon, Neptune

·•◊ CRYSTALS ◊•·
Moonstone, carnelian, larimar

·•◊ ZODIAC ◊•·
Pisces, Cancer, Scorpio

·•◊ COLOR ◊•·
Blue

·•◊ CARDINAL DIRECTION ◊•·
West

·•◊ ENERGY ◊•·
Feminine

The element of earth is represented in the Suit of Pentacles and speaks to our need for material wealth, physical comfort, and building a strong foundation. Earth is a slow-moving and methodical feminine energy. It asks you to get clear about what you need to feel safe and grounded so you can build a strong foundation for growth. The symbol of the Pentacle itself is a representation of earth. All four elements, with the addition of spirit, also called aether, are represented by each point of the star. As misunderstood as this symbol is, it is nothing more than an invocation of the five elements and is often used as a form of protection.

Energetically, earth calls you to get comfortable in your body, savor physical pleasures, and build strong foundations in your life. An earthy person will likely present as being very calm and stable, and someone who savors their physical senses. Someone lacking earth energy will appear flighty, anxious, and disconnected from their body. I'm sure, like me, you can imagine times when you've embodied each of these descriptions!

In nature, it's easy to observe the qualities of earth. The earth itself is our stable foundation for life. We build the foundations for our homes on the sturdy ground and are nurtured by the plentiful gifts of food from the earth. Nature takes care of us and always moves at its own pace.

··· ⸙ ···

ROOT YOURSELF FIRMLY INTO THE PRESENT MOMENT. THE PHYSICAL WORLD IS HERE TO SUPPORT YOU.

··· ⸙ ···

The Major Arcana cards associated with the element of earth are foundational, just like the element itself. When you master the element of earth and the cards associated with it, you'll find yourself in the space of deep appreciation for the physical world. You cannot grow spiritually until you have a firm foundation to build upon.

EARTH CORRESPONDENCES

TAROT MINOR ARCANA
Suit of Pentacles and the Pages

TAROT MAJOR ARCANA
Empress, Hierophant, Hermit, Devil, World

BODY
Sacrum

CHAKRA
Root

PLANETS
Earth, Venus, Saturn

CRYSTALS
Hematite, moss agate, garnet

ZODIAC
Taurus, Virgo, Capricorn

COLOR
Green, black

CARDINAL DIRECTION
North

ENERGY
Feminine

The fast-acting and communicative element of air comes to bring whispers and intuitive nudges of new beginnings. Air brings truth, inspiration, new ideas, and swift action. The Suit of Swords, not surprisingly, is associated with air. Swords move with swift precision to make changes, cut ties, and communicate clearly and sometimes quite sharply! In nature, air can be quite unpredictable. We know air is present all around us but don't always know how it will act.

Energetically, we see air manifest as a whisper or lightning bolt of inspiration, intuitive insights, and a desire to communicate truthfully. The element of air is responsible for ideas that seem to land in your mind from out of nowhere. The truth seeker with pleas to do what is right, not what is easy, is spurred on by the element of air. Air calls you into action in a way that brings forth divine truth.

BE OPEN TO NEW WAYS OF BEING AND
SEEING. INSPIRATION FROM SPIRIT
IS ALL AROUND.

Like all of the elements, the energy of air can manifest in both positive and negative ways. In nature, an abundance of air can come in the form of violent and destructive winds. Within our personalities, air can manifest as feeling flighty and anxious or as sharp and hurtful language. Because air is invisible and more unpredictable, it can feel harder to understand and a bit "all over the place." If needed, air can always be tempered with its opposite element, earth.

In the tarot, the Suit of Swords, ruled by air, can seem quite negative and shocking, but if you dig deeper, you can see a different story evolve. Air has the necessary but sometimes difficult task of bringing truth into our physical world. It also calls on us to take leaps of faith at times, even when it's scary. Air calls for extreme faith in the sometimes challenging process of living a purposeful life in alignment with your truth.

AIR CORRESPONDENCES

TAROT MINOR ARCANA
Suit of Swords and the Kings

TAROT MAJOR ARCANA
Fool, Magician, Lovers, Justice, Star

BODY
Throat, voice

CHAKRA
Throat

PLANETS
Mercury, Uranus

CRYSTALS
Kyanite, amethyst, sodalite

ZODIAC
Aquarius, Gemini, Libra

COLOR
Yellow

CARDINAL DIRECTION
East

ENERGY
Masculine

FIRE

The element of fire comes on strong to help you burn through what isn't serving you and take action toward your desires. In the Minor Arcana, we see fire represented in the Suit of Wands. A wand is a common tool used to manifest and direct energy, which is a perfect embodiment of the element of fire. Fire is the masculine counterpart to the feminine energy of water. Fire is fast-acting, assertive, energetic, and influential. While its counterpart, water, expresses its power through a sustained slow-moving force, a fire burns bright but often for a shorter period of time.

Energetically, fire can be seen in the person who always seems to have energy. The energetic nature of fire can come off as very charismatic, and those with very fiery personalities often find themselves in positions of power. Someone lacking the energy of fire may find it hard to act on their desires or lose steam on a project early on. When you find yourself digging deep for the inner resources to carry on, fire comes to help you complete the task at hand.

FAN THE FLAMES OF YOUR INTERNAL FIRE;
THE ENERGY YOU NEED IS WITHIN YOU.

In nature, fire has played a primary role in the evolution and expansion of the human species. Harnessing the power of fire gave us the ability to keep warm and cook food, and even overcome challenging environments. When fire catches hold of a dry forest, it seemingly destroys everything quite quickly. What we don't always understand is that the burning was a necessary part of regenerating the land.

Though fire does have destructive qualities, it has the power to bring you to a place of more wholeness. The Major Arcana associated with this element have a mixture of strength, joy, and destruction. Each of these aspects is necessary to continue to grow and expand. When you master the element of fire, you learn how to harness your energy and use it in meaningful ways.

···✮ FIRE CORRESPONDENCES ✮···

·●◊ TAROT MINOR ARCANA ◊●·
Suit of Wands and the Knights

·●◊ TAROT MAJOR ARCANA ◊●·
Emperor, Strength, Wheel of Fortune, Temperance, Tower, Sun, Judgment

·●◊ BODY ◊●·
Gut

·●◊ CHAKRA ◊●·
Solar plexus

·●◊ PLANETS ◊●·
Mars, Jupiter, Sun, Pluto

·●◊ CRYSTALS ◊●·
Pyrite, red jasper, citrine

·●◊ ZODIAC ◊●·
Aries, Leo, Sagittarius

·●◊ COLOR ◊●·
Red, orange

·●◊ CARDINAL DIRECTION ◊●·
South

·●◊ ENERGY ◊●·
Masculine

EXPERIENCING THE ELEMENTS IN THE TAROT

Try this exercise to become more familiar with the elements and the tarot. Spend a week exploring each suit of the Minor Arcana and their corresponding element. Look at the cards every day. Intuitively select one card to meditate on. Ask yourself how it relates to the element it is associated with. Add a couple of rituals for each element that you're working with for the week. Here are a few examples of ways to work with each element.

- ◆ **Cups and water**: Go for a swim, take a bath or a shower, enjoy a creative project like painting or drawing, set aside time to feel and express emotions, or get in touch with your intuition.

- ◆ **Pentacles and earth**: Go for a walk in nature, meditate sitting on the earth, garden, exercise, or prepare a meal for yourself from scratch.

- ◆ **Swords and air**: Start a new project, meditate with the intent to be open to new ideas, perform a new moon ritual, sing, or express yourself through writing or speaking.

- ♦ **Wands and fire**: Light a candle or enjoy a bonfire, play, exercise, pick up a project you put down or finish a project, or write a list of your favorite qualities.

Absorbing the wisdom of the four elements will give you a new lens to experience the world and the tarot. You'll begin seeing the elements manifest in your life and those around you and better understand how to balance these energies when needed. The four elements are a powerful stepping-stone toward understanding the tarot on a deeper level.

⋯☆ NUMEROLOGY ☆⋯

As with the four elements, there's a strong theme of numerology in the tarot. When you understand the basics of numerology, you'll increase your ability to intuitively read the cards. In this section, you'll learn the basic meanings of the numbers 1 to 10 and how to apply them to the Minor Arcana and Major Arcana.

As you move through these next two sections, keep in mind that numerology and astrology (which we'll get to soon) are massive topics. Even though we'll only be scratching the surface of these complex practices, it will be enough to take your tarot reading to the next level. Also, just like the four elements, you'll likely find that learning a bit about numerology will bolster other spiritual practices in your life.

Numerology is the belief that every number carries an energetic vibration. The energy of each number is used to gain insight into our personalities, life paths, and even the direction of humankind. Numbers cannot lie. No matter your background or faith, 2 + 2 will always equal 4. Numbers connect all of us, not only with each other but also with nature and the Universe.

NUMBERS ARE THE LANGUAGE OF THE UNIVERSE.

HOW NUMEROLOGY SHOWS
UP IN THE TAROT

I'm going to focus on the most common ways that numerology shows up in the tarot. Knowing the meaning of numbers 1 to 10 will be especially helpful when it comes to understanding tarot card meanings quickly. For the most part, you'll apply this to the numbered cards of the Minor Arcana. However, there are some basic ways to apply these numbers to the Major Arcana as well.

In the numbered Minor Arcana cards (cards 1 to 10), understanding the numbers helps each suit tell a story. You'll begin to see a theme between each of the suits based on the progression of the numbers. Add this together with your understanding of the four elements, and you've got a solid foundation for the meaning of each of the numbered pip cards.

In the Major Arcana, you can apply the same understanding of the number meanings. Traditionally in numerology, you'll add any double digits to reduce it down to a single-digit number. For example, if you're looking at the numerological meaning of the Justice card, which is number 11, you'd take 1 + 1 to reduce it down to the number 2. The numerological meaning of this card is pretty easy to make sense of because the number 2 is all about creating balance. Not all of them are quite as obvious, but you'll be able to glean some information from each of the Major Arcana cards using this technique.

You can take this technique a step further by taking into consideration the energy of the two numbers you're adding together and the order they're added together for double digits of the Major Arcana. For example, the number 3 is associated with the Empress (card 3), the Hanged One (card 12, 1+2=3), and the World (card 21, 2+1=3). Each card resonates with the number 3, but the energy of each card is slightly different due to the order of the numbers. Both the Hanged One and the World resonate with the number 3, 1, and 2, but the energy of the number 1 will be stronger in the Hanged One and the energy of the 2 will be stronger in the World because it's the first in the sequence.

Beyond this, there are also master numbers, karmic debt numbers you can opt to take into consideration while deciphering cards. Master numbers are special double-digit numbers used in numerology, including 11, 22, and 33. They can be deciphered as single digits (11 could also be deciphered as 1+1=2), but also have a unique vibration of their own as a double-digit master number. Karmic debt numbers including 13, 14, 16, and 19 are indicative of karmic lessons that need to be learned. The applications of numerology in deciphering the tarot are nearly endless!

Let's get started with learning the numbers.

⋯☆ NUMEROLOGY MEANINGS ☆⋯

0
Endless Potential + Wholeness

1
New Beginnings + Hope

2
Balance + Partnership

3
Creativity + Collaboration

4
Stability + Building Foundations

5
Change + Communication

6
Harmony + Equal Reciprocity

7
Strategy + Intellect

8
Mastery + Willpower

9
Fruition + Accomplishment

10
Completion + Moving On

⋯☆ NUMEROLOGY MEANINGS ☆⋯

◁〜 NUMBER 0 〜▷

Wholeness, potential, and the seed of life are themes of the number 0. All potentials are held within this number. This number is both everything and nothing, simultaneously. The Fool is the only card to hold this unique number, and the card's meaning mimics the meaning of this number perfectly. Anything and everything is possible with the number 0.

◁〜 NUMBER 1 〜▷

New beginnings, curiosity, openness, and hope are themes of this number. The number 1 indicates the start of a new cycle, a fresh start, a new project, or the beginning of a new evolution in your life journey. The number 1 often signals that it's time to get started on whatever you've been putting off. In a card reading, it might present when you need a nudge or need to be reminded to be open to new possibilities.

◁〜 NUMBER 2 〜▷

The number 2 signifies balance, partnership, loving relationships, and cooperation. It often indicates that some sort of partnership is coming your way; this doesn't necessarily mean a romantic relationship, but it could. Receiving a 2 in a reading, depending on the orientation of the card, may indicate that you're either in balance or out of balance. The number 2 also indicates the very early stages of a journey.

NUMBER 3

The number 3 signals creativity, creation, collaborations, harmony, and expressiveness. This is a very active number that indicates a deeply creative time. Number 3 usually represents very active energy, for better or worse. Receiving a 3 in a reading may be showing you that you need to take time for creativity. If you're feeling stuck in a process, it could also indicate a need to collaborate with others.

NUMBER 4

The number 4 marks a time of stability and strong foundations. This number often aligns with the ability to manifest new things because you've laid the groundwork. The number 4 often presents as being very grounded in reality, sometimes too much so. In a reading, a 4 may show up to commend you for laying a solid foundation or to pull you back to reality and remind you that you need more stability.

NUMBER 5

The number 5 likes to shake things up! The 5 is all about change, transitions, and communication. This is another active number. It's also quite unpredictable, as 5 often indicates a sudden and unexpected change. This number may show up in a reading to clue you into an upcoming change or to push you to make one, or it might indicate an argument, as it's closely tied to communication.

◁〜 NUMBER 6 〜▷

The number 6 is another harmonious number. It corresponds to being in harmony, caregiving, and equal reciprocity. The number 6 often presents in matters that involve family, friends, or work relationships. In a reading, a 6 may show up to highlight a situation that's out of balance or needs mending. It can also indicate that you're giving too much and need to take better care of yourself.

◁〜 NUMBER 7 〜▷

The number 7 represents strategy, mystery, spirituality, and intellect. This number may be one of the hardest to understand. The 7 often indicates a time of wanting or needing to grasp things. In the tarot, 7 may present as a call to be more contemplative or strategic.

◁〜 NUMBER 8 〜▷

The number 8 represents mastery, hard work, and willpower. This number often focuses on a need to master a skill or a trait and is aligned with manifesting. It presents to tell you that you've done what you need to, and it's time to take off in your skill. In the tarot, an 8 may show up to commend you for a job well done or spur you to continue on.

◁〜 NUMBER 9 〜▷

The number 9 deals with fruition, completing a goal, and savoring your efforts. It signals the end of a cycle is near but calls you to learn from the final stages of the process. A 9 shows up in a reading to remind you to enjoy the fruits of your labor, or alternatively, may indicate the calm before a storm.

◁〜 NUMBER 10 〜▷

Traditionally in numerology, the numbers 1 to 9 are the primary numbers, and any number over 9 is added together to make a single-digit number. In the case of the tarot, the number 10, not surprisingly, represents an end of a cycle. However, the 10 in the tarot goes beyond an ending. It also signifies a willingness or inner knowing that another cycle needs to begin.

⸱⸱⸱✮ ASTROLOGY ✮⸱⸱⸱

Astrology is the art of understanding how the position of stars, planets, and heavenly bodies affect each of us. Each constellation and planet is associated with different meanings and themes. Some people believe that astrology is foundational to understanding the tarot, while others don't study it at all. I believe it's worth knowing the primary themes of the twelve zodiac signs and planets while working with the tarot. Beyond these astrology basics, I'll leave it up to you whether or not you want to dive deeper.

HOW ASTROLOGY SHOWS UP IN THE TAROT

Because we've already discussed the four elements, you've been introduced to one way that astrology shows up in the cards. Each element corresponds to three different zodiac signs, and you already know that the elements are a big part of the tarot. Check out the correspondence guides in the elements section (starting on page 26) to refresh your memory about the elements and the zodiac. In the Major Arcana, each card is associated with a zodiac sign or planet. Remember, these cards are the big players of the tarot, so it's not surprising that they're assigned extra meanings and correspondences. Because tarot and astrology each have such a long history, it's not uncommon to see the cards and astrology correspond differently in some places. If you see someone using different planetary or zodiac correspondences for different cards, it doesn't necessarily mean that they're wrong; they might just have a different practice, and that's okay!

Here's a list of commonly associated Major Arcana tarot cards and their astrological counterparts.

- ◆ **0. The Fool**: Uranus

- ◆ **1. The Magician**: Mercury

- ◆ **2. The High Priestess**: The Moon

- ◆ **3. The Empress**: Venus

- ◆ **4. The Emperor**: Aries

- ◆ **5. The Hierophant**: Taurus

- ◆ **6. The Lovers**: Gemini

- ◆ **7. The Chariot**: Cancer

- ◆ **8. Strength**: Leo

- ◆ **9. The Hermit**: Virgo

- ◆ **10. Wheel of Fortune**: Jupiter

- ◆ **11. Justice**: Libra

- ◆ **12. The Hanged One**: Neptune

- ◆ **13. Death**: Scorpio

♦ **14. Temperance**: Sagittarius

♦ **15. The Devil**: Capricorn

♦ **16. The Tower**: Mars

♦ **17. The Star**: Aquarius

♦ **18. The Moon**: Pisces

♦ **19. The Sun**: The Sun

♦ **20. Judgment**: Pluto

♦ **21. The World**: Saturn

To help make sense of all of these astrological correspondences, check out the graphics on pages 56 and 57 for general meanings for each zodiac sign and planet.

·◦◭ TIP ◮◦·

Take your correspondence knowledge a step further by learning the corresponding elements for each zodiac sign. Aries, Leo, and Sagittarius correspond with fire. Taurus, Virgo, and Capricorn correspond with earth. Gemini, Libra, and Aquarius correspond with air. Cancer, Scorpio, and Pisces correspond with water.

As far as the Minor Arcana goes, you can certainly apply your understanding of the zodiac in the elements, as we discussed above. Astrology weaves its way through the Minor Arcana in other ways, but it starts to get pretty complicated. If you're loving this section on astrology and want to dive deeper into how it plays out in the tarot, I definitely suggest doing so!

Think of all of this as different ways to layer more meaning and understanding into each card of the tarot. The more deeply you understand the elements, numerology, and astrology, the more it will enhance your depth of understanding the tarot. You'll begin to see each card as layered energies, which is how they're meant to be experienced.

Understanding these correspondences will also give your intuition a starting place. I like to think of them as a springboard for intuition. For example, if you lay out a spread with loads of Cups, it gives you an idea that this reading will deal with themes associated with the element of water.

Now that you have a foundation of each card's energies let's learn some ways to start using your deck.

GENERAL PLANETARY MEANINGS

SUN
The ego, strength, outward-facing personality

MOON
The subconscious, emotions, shadow side

MERCURY
Communication, intelligence, intellect

VENUS
Love, relationships, balance

MARS
War, power, leadership

JUPITER
Expansion, growth, happiness

SATURN
Stability, restriction, structure

URANUS
Disobedience, revolution, eccentricity

NEPTUNE
Fantasy, dreams, spirituality

PLUTO
Destruction, transformation

GENERAL ZODIAC MEANINGS

ARIES
Ruled by Mars, go-getter + bold

TAURUS
Ruled by Venus, stable + driven

GEMINI
Ruled by Mercury, communicative + adaptable

CANCER
Ruled by the moon, sensitive + gentle

LEO
Ruled by the sun, outgoing + confident

VIRGO
Ruled by Mercury, logical + grounded

LIBRA
Ruled by Venus, balanced + caring

SCORPIO
Ruled by Pluto, deep + intense

SAGITTARIUS
Ruled by Jupiter, adventurous + ambitious

CAPRICORN
Ruled by Saturn, hardworking + responsible

AQUARIUS
Ruled by Uranus, truth seeker + eccentric

PISCES
Ruled by Neptune, intuitive + creative

CHAPTER 3

USING AND READING THE CARDS

The number one tip I'll share with you is to start working with the tarot right away. You don't have to wait until you know the multiple and layered meanings of every card to begin working with your deck. In fact, I'd advise against it. That's not to say that I think you should start charging folks for readings right away (I don't!), but there are many other ways to work with the cards besides doing paid readings.

One of the best things about working with the tarot is that you'll begin to form your own relationships with the cards as you work with them. What each card means to you is a very personal thing that you'll develop alongside your intuition. It's also important to keep in mind that your relationship with each card will change over time. The tarot is not a fixed tool. It's fluid, and the more you work with it, the more obvious this will become.

In this chapter, you'll learn various ways to use tarot cards (besides readings), the basics about getting started with reading tarot cards, different ways to interpret them, and the role your intuition plays. I'll also debunk some common myths.

·•◊ TIP ◊•·

As you read through the different ways you can work with tarot cards, notice which one calls to you the most. It's likely the best place to start your tarot journey!

DIFFERENT WAYS TO
WORK WITH THE CARDS

Like I've said, having infallible psychic abilities is not a prerequisite for working with the tarot. No matter your intuitive skill level, jump on in! The more you work with tarot as a personal growth tool, the more your intuition will improve and expand. I believe they go hand in hand. Be open to different ways of working with the tarot. The options are truly endless. The tarot is a deep well of wisdom that I can assure you will never run dry! The following are a few ways to work with the tarot.

JOURNALING

Journal about the tarot cards, especially the cards of the Major Arcana. As I mentioned in chapter 1, the Major Arcana cards reflect the most common experiences of the human condition. For example, the Devil card, among other things, represents our deepest desires and the things we rarely talk about. We've all had the very human experience of desiring something we view as forbidden.

Here are some suggestions for questions to ask yourself when you're journaling about different cards:

- How does this card make me feel?

- What symbols or imagery jumps out to me?

- Are there any archetypes or human themes that stand out to me in this card?

- How does this card show up in my life right now?

- What can I learn from this card?

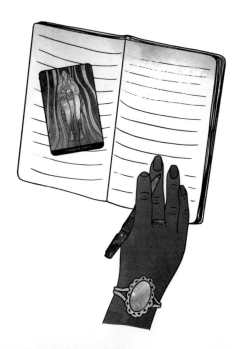

SELF-REFLECTION AND PERSONAL GROWTH READINGS

Perform readings for yourself or others to clarify the present moment or current situation. For this use, try to think of the tarot as a dear friend that you're turning to for advice, rather than a fortune-telling device. Pull one card or more. Use a spread below if you'd like. Ask yourself what the card(s) you selected have to say about you and how you're reacting to what's happening. Look to the cards to uncover themes or ideas you may be avoiding, the deeper purpose of the situation, or what you have to learn from the situation.

ENERGY READINGS

Everything is energy, and it connects us to each other and the Universe. The tarot is a great tool for working with energy or assessing your or another's energy. When you work with the cards specifically to assess your energy, each card acts as a signal that you either have too much or too little of that energy. For example, if you pull some cards to determine what your energy needs to be more balanced and you pull loads of Pentacles, that would be a sign that you need more grounding in your life to feel more balanced because the Pentacles relate to the element of earth.

◄◡ SHADOW WORK ◡►

Shadow work is the practice of intentionally exploring difficult and scary parts of life so you can integrate them to become more whole. The cards of the tarot contain a complete range of human experiences. It does not gloss over the hard, scary, and sometimes earth-shattering parts of life. Your cards will not shield you from your shadow. Instead, they call you to cozy up to your shadow to understand better what it has to teach you. Here are a few ways to dive into shadow work using your tarot card deck.

♦ Journal about the cards that make you the most uncomfortable. Use the questions from the earlier journaling section.

♦ Ask questions specifically to explore your shadow, like:

    ◊ What parts of my shadow need healing and exploring?

    ◊ What do I have to learn from my shadow?

    ◊ What parts of my shadow have I been avoiding?

◁◠ UNDERSTANDING COMMON ARCHETYPES ◠▷

The tarot, especially the Major Arcana, is full of common archetypes. Archetypes are timeless and universal energies that are understood across cultures. For example, the archetype of the mother is something we can all understand on some level. Even if you do not have a relationship with your biological mother or have children of your own, the overarching energy of the archetype of the mother is something you can understand. Furthermore, you do not have to be a mother or a woman to embody the mother's archetype. Anyone can access and learn from the energy of motherhood.

The way the archetypes show up can be personal and vary from person to person. Here are some of the archetypes I associate with the cards: the ego (the Sun), Soul (the Moon), mother (Empress), father (Emperor), wizard (Magician), child (the Fool), lover (the Lovers), martyr (Hanged One), seer (Hermit), and authoritarian (Hierophant), etc. You may decide on different archetypal associations with different cards, and that's fine. To work with the archetypes, explore how the archetypal energies associated with the cards make you feel, look at the symbology on each card and explore how it makes you feel about its archetype, or journal about the cards and their archetypal connections.

MAGICK AND SPELLWORK

Because each tarot card carries a unique energy, they are perfect for adding energy and intention to spellwork, magick, and your altar. You can do this by placing a card on your altar to invite in a specific kind of energy. For example, if you're focusing on improving your intuition, you could place the Moon, the High Priestess, or the Queen of Cups on your altar as a reminder and energetic intention. Or, add a card to a spell to layer in an additional King of Energy. For example, if you're focusing on bringing more abundance into your life, you could include the Nine of Pentacles or the Empress into your spell.

DIVINATION

You can certainly use the tarot as a tool to glean insights about the future. Psychics have been successfully using the tarot for this purpose for centuries. The best way to get started is to start reading for yourself and others regularly with the intent to connect with psychic energy. Don't skip this last step; it's really the only difference between some of the above methods! I'll dive deeper into using your intuition for card readings in the next section.

WAYS TO READ THE CARDS

Not surprisingly, there are also several techniques to try when it comes to reading your cards. You do not need to master all of the techniques I mention to work with your tarot cards. The very act of working with your cards regularly, in any way that feels good to you, will help you become more familiar with the cards and teach you new ways to learn from them.

Here's a list of common ways to read and interpret the cards.

- Intuitive card readings

- Using a guidebook

- Understanding common correspondences within the tarot

- Letting the cards tell a story

You can use any combination of the above methods to decipher the cards you pull. I tell you this because I don't want you to feel like you have to memorize all of the correspondences to start working with the tarot. You can start out relying solely on your intuition and build from there.

This is the beautiful thing about working with tarot, there's no right way to work with the cards. There are endless ways to layer more meaning into your readings and there's nothing wrong with using a guidebook. I suggest trying out several different techniques, to determine where your strengths lie.

YOUR INTUITION AND
THE TAROT

As I said earlier, humans have been using their intuition to predict the future since the beginning of time. This isn't something unique to the tarot. However, the tarot does happen to be a great tool to do this. If your primary goal is to work with the tarot as a divination tool, I suggest getting comfortable with all of the methods outlined earlier. Secondly, you'll want to get very familiar with how you receive intuitive and psychic information.

The way we each process and receive psychic information varies greatly. Some of us hear things in our minds, see visions in our minds, or have an inner knowing. All are correct and valid. In a tarot reading, this could present as seeing or hearing things about the cards in your mind or having an inner knowing about the querent (or yourself) as you look at the cards. You will be weaving together the story, symbols, and meanings of the cards in front of you in the same way you would for any other reading, with the addition of connecting to a source greater than yourself to gain insights into the future for yourself or the reader.

If you feel like you need extra support in the intuition arena, check out page 68 for some suggestions to jump-start your intuitive abilities.

WAYS TO INSPIRE
YOUR INTUITION

Work with your tarot
cards daily.

Meditate for 10 to
15 minutes a day.

Learn techniques to
open the third eye.

Tune in to your
breath and body.

Work with crystals that inspire
intuition, like amethyst,
labradorite, and kyanite.

Make connections
with your spirit
guides and ancestors.

⋯☆ INTUITIVE CARD READINGS ☆⋯

Some who work with the tarot choose to rely solely on their intuition, this is called intuitive tarot reading. This can be a great technique to help you wean yourself off of a guidebook and hone your intuitive abilities. Here is how you can give intuitive tarot readings a try.

- ◆ Spend a couple minutes grounding yourself and connecting to your breath.

- ◆ Pull one or more cards and lay them out in front of you.

- ◆ Ask yourself: What symbols, colors, and emotions do I notice? What is standing out to me?

- ◆ Pay close attention to sensations in your body as you look at the cards. Are there any feelings or sensations you're experiencing as you look at the cards in front of you?

- ◆ Allow yourself to be guided entirely by your intuitive nudges to decipher the cards.

Working with the cards in this way allows you to jump in right away and it also requires you to get very comfortable working with your intuition.

UNDERSTANDING
STORIES IN THE TAROT

When you understand the basic roles of the different kinds of cards in the tarot, it will help stories unfold in your readings. Here are common ways that the cards manifest themselves in readings.

- **Major Arcana** - Reference big life themes and the common archetypes we all work through.

- **Minor Arcana** - Offer guidance on day-to-day happenings and how you interact with those around you.

- **Court cards** - Signal important people in your life (Pages usually represent children, Knights – teens, Queens – mother figures, and Kings – father figures).

As we already discussed, the cards of the Major Arcana tell a story called "The Fool's Journey." You'll find that stories emerge within each of the suits of the Minor Arcana too. When you begin to see how the cards relate to each other in a bigger picture, it will add another layer to deciphering the cards. The stories the cards tell may be incredibly personal to you and guided by intuition. This is yet another optional tool in your tarot reading toolbox.

⋯☆ READING REVERSED CARDS ☆⋯

Reversed cards are cards that appear upside down in your readings. Some who work with the tarot use reversed cards and some do not. Both options are valid. When just starting out, you might find it helpful to save reversed card meanings until you start to feel more comfortable with the cards. I'd also like to point out that reversed card meanings are not inherently bad, this is yet another tarot myth! Some simply interpret reversed cards to mean the opposite of the upright meaning, but there are other ways to work with them. You'll want to use your intuition to determine how each reversed card needs to be deciphered for you. Here are a few of my favorite ways to interpret reversed cards.

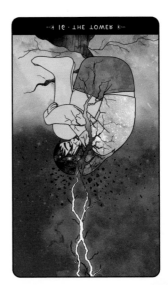

- ◆ Reversed cards may indicate that the energy of the card is being expressed internally, rather than outwardly.

- ◆ A reversed card may correspond to an energy that is being suppressed or blocked, either consciously or unconsciously.

- ◆ Reversed cards can also indicate growth opportunities for yourself or those you're reading for.

DIFFICULT READINGS AND "BAD" CARDS

When you do have the inevitable reading that seems difficult or is off for you or the querent, don't let it deter you. You'll have off days (we all do!), and sometimes the person you're reading for could have an energetic block preventing you from reading their cards. This is part of the process. It's also helpful to remember that the reading may not make sense at the time. Trust that in the days and weeks ahead, it will become clearer.

Before we get into the card spreads, let's clear up any concerns you may have about pulling a "bad" or "scary" card. It's going to happen eventually, and I don't want you to let it ruin your day.

YOU HAVE FREE WILL AND WILL ALWAYS HAVE FREE WILL. THE CARDS ARE NOT YOUR FATE.

Pulling the Death (Devil, Tower, etc.) card doesn't mean you're going to die tomorrow or that your life will fall apart. Every card in the tarot has layered meanings. For example, the Death card usually signifies a transformation of sorts, and certainly not always a bad one (although, let's be honest, not all transitions are fun).

Don't worry. You'll learn all about the layered meaning of each card later on.

Going through difficult times is part of being human and growing. Growth makes us better, or at the very least, gives us tools to help others going through a similar situation. So, even if one of your scary card pulls does come true, trust that it's for your highest good in the long run. Can you think of something difficult that happened in your life that eventually landed you in an even better situation? I know I can.

If you didn't receive the message you were hoping for or expecting, wait a few days and look for signs. You'll often find that the message you received was exactly what you needed, and it will usually make itself apparent. If you wait a few days and the message is still vague, try clearing your mind with a short meditation and asking your higher self or spirit guides to make the message clearer, and then do another card spread.

The suggestions in this chapter are not to make you feel overwhelmed. I offer them to help you feel empowered to work with your tarot cards in ways that feel meaningful to you. You do not need to work with the cards in all of the ways I mention or master all of the different techniques. Start with the suggestions that feel exciting and natural to you, and trust that you'll know when it's time to layer in a new technique!

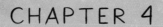

CHAPTER 4

CARD SPREADS

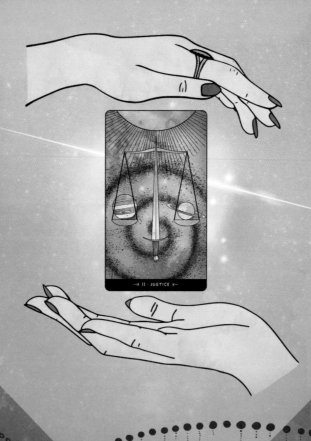

Just like your tarot cards, card spreads do not need to be relegated to divination. You can use the card spreads outlined in this chapter (and others) for self-exploration, shadow work, energy readings, or journaling practice. Working with card spreads is a powerful way for the cards to speak to you in stories. The stories you form from different spreads can then be used as learning tools or for divination. Working with the cards in this way will help you develop a deeper relationship with your cards. With each spread you do, you'll see new themes emerge and better understand how different cards work together.

Another idea I'd like you to keep in mind is that your card spreads can be fluid. Think of any card spread you use as a starting point. Don't hesitate to build onto a card reading anytime you feel called. This could mean pulling a few additional cards in different areas of a spread to gain more clarity. Furthermore, you don't need to master long or elaborate spreads to work with tarot cards. Start where you feel most comfortable and then progress from there. Before we dive into different card spreads, let's discuss a couple of techniques to help you select your cards for readings.

⋯☆ CARD SELECTION TECHNIQUES ☆⋯

When it comes to using your intuition, knowing when to stop shuffling the deck and flip cards over can feel like an important task. It is important, but not as important as you might have it built it up to be in your head. I've outlined a couple of ways to help you intuitively select cards in the following sections. Ultimately, it's important to trust the cards you receive and find ways to connect them to yourself or the reader using all of your tarot-reading tools.

◁⌣ THE RAINBOW TECHNIQUE ⌣▷

Spread your cards out. Slowly move your hands over your cards. Tune in to your body and ask Spirit to give you a signal in your body when it's the right card. You might feel a tingle in your fingers or hand, have a gut knowing, or some other physical experience. Whatever it is, trust it, and select the card. You'll eventually develop a rapport with your intuition and know how it speaks to you. This technique works well for one-to-three-card spreads but can be time consuming if you plan to do a larger card spread.

THE SHUFFLE TECHNIQUE

Begin shuffling your cards. Ask Spirit for a sign to indicate when you should stop. This could come from hearing "stop" in your mind, receiving an inner knowing, or a sensation in your body when it's time for you to stop. When you sense something, trust it, and flip the top card over. You can continue flipping cards from the top or reshuffle for each card selection. This method works well for multiple-card spreads, as you can flip over as many cards as you need off the top.

·◦◊ TIP ◊◦·

**When reading for others, you can have them
shuffle or cut the deck for themselves.**

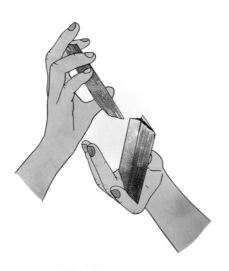

Here are five different tarot card spreads to help you get more comfortable reading the cards for yourself and others. There are endless ways to create card spreads. You absolutely do not have to stick with the ones I outline here. In fact, you can even create your own by need, and I include steps for doing that at the end of this chapter.

THE ONE-CARD PULL

The one-card pull is a great way to get comfortable with your tarot cards. Try asking your cards a question every day and intuitively selecting one card. It could be something as simple as, "What should I focus on today?" "How can I be of service to others today?" or "What message does Spirit have for me today?"

One-card spreads can also be used as an easy "yes" or "no" guidance system. If you use your deck in this way, it will act similar to a pendulum in its answers. Be careful to only ask your deck questions that would have a "yes" or "no" answer when using it for this purpose. In many tarot practices, the cards are each associated with "yes," "no," or "maybe." The way people boil down yes/no answers in the tarot can really vary, so I suggest using your intuition. However, if this method speaks to you, you can investigate the different yes/no meanings of each of the cards that others have laid out.

THE CARDS
DON'T LIE.

THREE-CARD SPREAD

The three-card spread is the most common and versatile of all of the card spreads. It is easy, has many uses, and can be applied to nearly any situation. This is a great card spread to master because it will help you feel more comfortable with larger card readings. The three-card spread allows you to see stories between the cards as they unfold and can help you connect their different meanings. See several three-card spread examples on the opposite page. View these as a mere starting point, as the options for three-card spreads are truly endless!

Three-card spreads are a great way to get comfortable journaling about your card reading and reading cards for others. When you journal about your readings, new themes and ideas will be uncovered. Journaling about your three-card spreads will give you a deeper insight into what the cards have to say.

THREE-CARD SPREAD
SUGGESTIONS

- ◆ Past, present, future

- ◆ Mind, body, spirit

- ◆ Problem, solution, outcome

- ◆ Personality, life path, potential

- ◆ Desire, hurdle, culmination

- ◆ You, your partner, your path together

- ◆ Your finances, your financial goals, financial blocks

- ◆ Shadow to integrate, how to integrate, growth opportunity

- ◆ Current job, barrier, new job

ENERGY REPORT SPREAD

As I mentioned above, the tarot, like all intuitive tools, can also be used as an energy-reading tool. In my personal practice, I like to work with the seven primary energy centers. Energy centers can be found referenced in cultures around the world, but you may be more familiar with the term chakras, which is rooted in ancient Vedic texts from India. The seven central energy points start at the base of your spine and end at the top of your head. Each energy point corresponds to different aspects of your life, energy, personality, and physical body. Refer to the next page for a quick overview of these energy centers and what they correspond to.

For this reading, you'll select one card for each energy center. You'll better understand what is going on in each chakra based on your reading. For example, if you select the Ace of Swords for the root chakra, this may indicate that you need to engage with the element of air to find a sense of balance and that you might be due for a change in your physical surroundings.

·•◌ TIP ◌•·

Using your knowledge of the four elements in the tarot will be helpful for working with them for energy readings. Each energy center corresponds to an element and can be useful when determining the status of each chakra.

···✮ ENERGY REPORT SPREAD ✮···

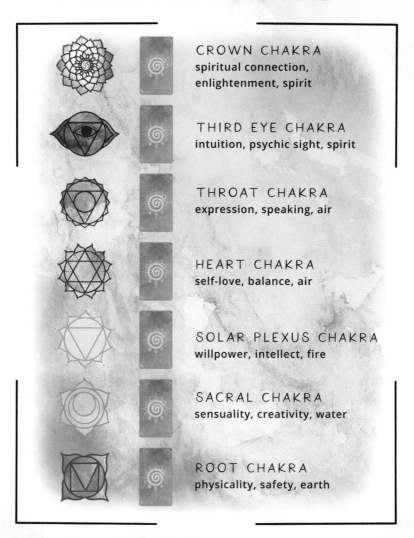

CROWN CHAKRA
spiritual connection, enlightenment, spirit

THIRD EYE CHAKRA
intuition, psychic sight, spirit

THROAT CHAKRA
expression, speaking, air

HEART CHAKRA
self-love, balance, air

SOLAR PLEXUS CHAKRA
willpower, intellect, fire

SACRAL CHAKRA
sensuality, creativity, water

ROOT CHAKRA
physicality, safety, earth

SIX-CARD JOURNEY SPREAD

This is a unique card spread I created to help you understand your journey here in physical form. It goes with my tarot card deck, *Journey Tarot*, but it can be used with any deck of your choosing. To perform this card spread, you'll select one card for each question below.

- ◆ How can I inspire spiritual growth?

- ◆ What is my biggest soul lesson?

- ◆ Where will I find the most joy?

- ◆ How can I best honor my journey?

- ◆ How can I best share my gifts with others?

- ◆ What is my primary purpose during my journey?

TIP

This card spread is ideal to practice on a full moon because it offers a unique energy of expansion, growth, and intuitive insights.

⋯✫ SIX-CARD JOURNEY SPREAD ✫⋯

TWELVE-MONTH SPREAD

One of my favorite ways to work with the tarot is to do a twelve-month card spread for the year ahead. Every year I do this, my tarot calendar always has new wisdom to share with me, and it's usually right on point for how my year goes. Remember, you always have free will, so if something comes up in your twelve-month tarot spread, try not to let it freak you out!

You can perform a twelve-month spread whenever you want. You don't have to wait until the New Year to practice this. Go ahead and pull cards for the rest of the year or do all twelve now. The cards and your intuition know where you're at. If you do have the foresight to do this around New Year's, that's great too. I like to wait for the first new moon of the year.

Center yourself and select a card for each month of the year ahead. I suggest writing down the cards you pull for the year ahead on one piece of paper so you can put it up somewhere you'll see it regularly. I place mine next to my calendar. You could also integrate the cards you pull for each month into your calendar or journal.

···☆ TWELVE-MONTH SPREAD ☆···

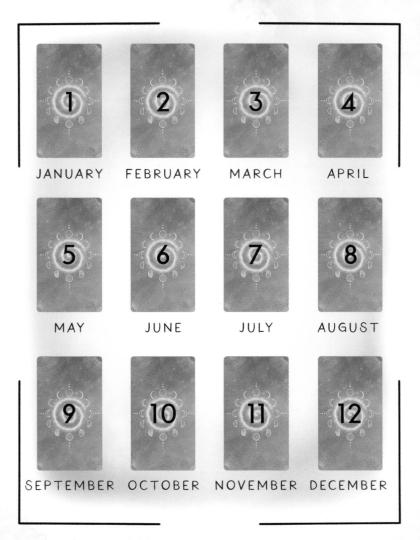

JANUARY   FEBRUARY   MARCH   APRIL

MAY   JUNE   JULY   AUGUST

SEPTEMBER   OCTOBER   NOVEMBER   DECEMBER

CREATING YOUR OWN
CARD SPREADS

Can't find a card spread for your exact need? Creating your own is a perfectly acceptable and highly intuitive option.

> ·•◊ TIP ◊•·
>
> **Want a new card spread but don't feel like creating one on your own? Search online for "card spread for [enter purpose (full moon, relationship advice, summer solstice, etc.)] and you'll be greeted with loads of options!**

If you do want to create your own card spread, follow these steps. You'll need your trusty tarot card deck, a writing utensil, and paper.

1. Write a list of questions about your query. Write everything that you're thinking about without judging. You won't need to use everything you write.

2. Looking at your list of questions, select the ones that feel most in line with your request. You'll also find it helpful to focus on open-ended questions if it's a larger reading. Yes and no questions work well for a one-card pull but can be very limiting in a larger card spread.

3. Select a number in line with your questions (check out the number meanings on pages 47 to 51 for help with this) or just pull cards until you feel called to stop.

4. If you'd like to take your card spread a step further, you can think about placing your cards in a specific shape that's unique to your question. For example, an upward-facing triangle to represent the fire element or a question pertaining to energy and action, or a downward-facing triangle to represent the water element or a question pertaining to intuition and the subconscious.

5. In your journal, write or sketch the shape of your card reading, how many cards you use, and the questions you'll be asking before you start your card reading.

6. Take a moment to center yourself, and you're ready to begin your unique card spread.

There are endless options for working with the tarot and performing card readings. There are card spreads like the Celtic cross that have been tried and tested for ages, but your unique spreads are just as valuable. Trust your inner guidance system when it comes to learning from the tarot, and you can't go wrong.

CHAPTER 5

THE MAJOR
ARCANA

The Major Arcana of the tarot speaks to life lessons, universal archetypes, and meaningful moments. When these cards come into your awareness, they're not to be ignored. They are always significant. The lessons from the Major Arcana cards have the power to go far beyond a message for a reading and are an invitation to learn, grow, and transform.

These cards come with layered meanings that can be highly unique to each person. Their symbology, associated archetypes, and correspondences all factor into their unique and layered meaning. Remember, the Major Arcana also tells a story. So, the card's location amidst "The Fool's Journey" is a relevant part of interpreting each card.

As with all of my card meaning suggestions, take what you like and leave the rest. If a personal meaning feels more accurate for you, honor it. Your intuitive voice is just as valid as my offerings.

⋯☆ 0. THE FOOL ☆⋯

The energy of the Fool is one of pure openness and wonder. This card calls to the childlike nature of your spirit. You're walking forward, arms outstretched, with stars in your eyes, and don't have a care in the world. This card is calling you to fully embody the energy of the Fool. Perhaps you already have the internal whispers of this sensation about a new journey. Alternatively, this card may be calling you to find a sense of wonderment and openness in an area of your life. The Fool's journey is not always one of joy and cheer, but the Fool doesn't care. The Fool's ability to walk into any situation with an inquisitive mind and heart is the true nature of this card. Can you find ways to embody the energy as you embark on new adventures, even if you know the path ahead may be rocky?

◁⌣ THE FOOL REVERSED ⌣▷

The reversed energy of the Fool indicates an unwillingness to move ahead or a feeling of being stuck. You may be in a forced state of stagnation, too afraid of what might lie ahead. Remember, life is a mixed bag of joy, and you came here to grow. Alternatively, this card reversed could show that you're being dangerously naive. Can you find ways to balance your desire for change and growth before floating off into the unknown?

⋯☆ 1. THE MAGICIAN ☆⋯

The Magician embodies all four elements: earth, air, water, and fire. The Magician understands that they have every tool they need at their fingertips and infinite ability to tap into them. This card calls you to notice all of the power you have. How can you make use of your divine gifts and use them for positive change for yourself and others? The energy of this card is one of mastery, willpower, and resourcefulness. The Magician may be calling you to dig deep for the strength and power you need to make powerful changes in your life or the world. This energy is not only about using your resources but also directing them with skill. Ruled by Mercury, the Magician also knows how to communicate clearly to effectively share their knowledge and wisdom with others.

◁⌣ THE MAGICIAN REVERSED ⌣▷

The energy of the Magician reversed could indicate a couple of things. It could mean to show you that you're blinding yourself from all of the tools you have nearby. Have you found yourself stuck with a sense of hopelessness? Can you find ways to work with what you have? Alternatively, this card's energy reversed could indicate that you're overusing your power in harmful ways. Understand that whatever you put out into the world will come back to you eventually.

⋯☆ 2. THE HIGH PRIESTESS ☆⋯

The High Priestess is a powerful call for you to connect with the beyond. You came from Source Energy and are always connected to the spirit realm, your guides, and your ancestors. This card is calling you to reconnect with this side. Be open to new ways to connect with Spirit and your natural intuitive gifts. Beyond the spirit realm, the High Priestess also calls you to acknowledge your subconscious. We cannot become one without full integration. Understanding and working with your shadow is a necessary part of becoming whole and honoring the depth of your mystical abilities. Don't shy away from the difficult or scary aspects of your being. Rather, embrace them and hold them closer to heal them. The High Priestess is ruled by the moon, so this card could also be calling you to connect with Mother Moon in more meaningful ways.

⋅◁〜 THE HIGH PRIESTESS REVERSED 〜▷⋅

The High Priestess reversed could indicate that you've cut yourself off from the spirit world and intuitive gifts, either intentionally or unintentionally. If you believe that you don't have intuition or feel as though you can't trust it, it's time to reconsider. If working with your intuition is new to you, you've been initiated, and it's time to start the journey. There may be important information being withheld from you if you're unwilling to receive it.

⭐ 3. THE EMPRESS ⭐

The Empress is the divine mother and supreme caregiver of the tarot. The energy of this card calls you to find deep reverence for nature and your physical vessel. The earth is the ultimate source of life and physical creation and should be honored with great regard. The Empress's energy calls you to find deep joy in physical creation and to birth new projects, ideas, or possibly a child. The Empress is fertile ground for your desires.

The Empress is ruled by Venus, the planet of love and attraction. This energy calls you to find ways to honor your body and indulge in the physical senses. This card may also be calling you to bring something new into the world.

THE EMPRESS REVERSED

The Empress reversed is a sign that you've been neglecting your physical body or the world around you. This card can come up if you've been spending too much time in the upper realms of spiritual energy. Remember, you are a physical being at the moment, even if spiritual at heart. It's important to honor and care for your body and nature at large. Alternatively, this card could be signaling a drought period of creative ideas, love, or fertility. How can you find small ways to work more creativity, love, and pleasure into your life to come back to the full energy of the Empress?

···✩ 4. THE EMPEROR ✩···

The Emperor represents divine masculine energy associated with leadership, power, and the ability to accomplish any goal. The energy of this card is stable and powerful. The zodiac sign associated with the Emperor is Aries, or the ram. The horns of the mighty ram indicate the ability to see any plan through to the end. Though the energy is fiery and intense, it is also stable and fatherly. The energy of the Emperor comes into your life to bring you strength and stability. If you're working diligently toward a goal, this card may appear to give you the strength you need to see it through. Alternatively, it may indicate a need to embody a more fatherly role in your life, bringing needed stability to you or those around you. It may benefit you to bring more structure into your life to accomplish your goals.

◄◡ THE EMPEROR REVERSED ◡►

This card's reversed energy indicates that you may be overusing your force in ways that are causing harm to you or those around you. The fiery nature of this card can easily become addictive or turn into unhealthy workaholism. Alternatively, this reversed card could also indicate a total lack of power and a feeling of extreme vulnerability. If this is the case, what's something small you can do to feel more empowered?

⭐ 5. THE HIEROPHANT ⭐

This traditionally religious card is a call to seek out spiritual guidance for sources rooted in wisdom and deep knowledge. If organized religion speaks to you, you can go that route as well. If it doesn't, seek the ancestral wisdom you resonate with most. If you've been learning on your own in an area of your life, this card is calling you to pause and build a stronger foundation through someone who's gone before you. Ruled by stable Taurus, this card wants to know that you are infinite beyond belief, but there's no substitute for learning from those with more experience. This card could also indicate interactions with established structures.

⤙ THE HIEROPHANT REVERSED ⤚

When the Hierophant appears reversed, it could indicate you're unwilling to learn from others or have shut yourself off from deep wisdom. If this is the case, it will be in your best interest to find a teacher or source with which you feel more in line. Alternatively, the reversed nature of this card could indicate that you're being extremely rigid or arrogant in your beliefs and unwilling to look at any source of external knowledge. If this is the case, this card is calling you to let go of your stubbornness.

⋯✬ 6. THE LOVERS ✬⋯

Though this card can undoubtedly signal new love, partnership, or romance, the wisdom of the Lovers is much deeper than earthly relationships. It also signals a need to make an important decision. The decision you make will ultimately lead to more or less harmony in your life. Are there any important decisions looming in your life that could bring you closer to a place of balance and peace? The Lovers card is ruled by Gemini, and this airy sign often indicates a busy mind with many options at the ready. The Lovers calls you to sit with your options to find the best and most harmonious decision for you and those around you. The choices you make will likely have lasting effects far into the future. Listen to your higher self and trust your intuition.

◁〰 THE LOVERS REVERSED 〰▷

The reversed nature of this card could signal impending trouble in a relationship. It also asks you to reflect on any choices you've been putting off or neglecting. Alternatively, this card reversed could be trying to tell you that you're rushing a decision and moving too fast in an area of your life. Remember, the decision this card calls forth will have lasting effects on your life. Proceed with caution and take your time.

···✦ 7. THE CHARIOT ✧···

The Chariot signals swift changes and a need to go with the flow. With the Lovers card we saw a call to make an important decision, and this card says that the wheels are in motion. The Chariot is ruled by watery and sensitive Cancer energy. These correspondences indicate that there's a deep need to flow with your emotions and not let yourself get caught up in them. Seek balance as you move forward, trusting that everything will work out in the end. You're always guided and surrounded by Spirit. As new experiences whirl into your world, greet them with grace and ease, then make a clear move. Dance through each new opportunity with clarity and deep trust that you have perfect control.

◄〜 THE CHARIOT REVERSED 〜►

When the Chariot appears reversed, it often signals an inability to move forward. Due to the Cancer energy associated with this card, the feeling of being stuck likely has to do with your emotions. It's time to find a way to work through your emotions so you can move forward. Alternatively, the reversed expression of this card could be telling you that you've released control over your life and are wandering around aimlessly. It may be time to gain some clarity about your path.

⋯✮ 8. STRENGTH ✮⋯

Strength comes in a variety of forms. Regardless of the form, when the Strength card presents, its energy has the power to change the world. This card calls you to be strong, and more importantly, to understand what strength looks like to you. Strength is ruled by the bold and bright sign of Leo. Leo reminds us to step into our power to inspire those around us. Are there areas where you've been holding yourself back? Now is the time to release any doubt or fears and let your voice be heard and your beauty seen. You're being called to face a situation with courage. This card also speaks to lust and carnal desires. Are there cravings that you've held yourself back from? Perhaps this card is calling you to face these desires head-on. Your strength, desires, and ability to shine are infinite.

◁◠ STRENGTH REVERSED ◠▷

This card's reversed nature implies that you may be avoiding something that you're scared to do or say. This card is an important call to stand up for what is right and what you believe in. Even if your voice shakes, it's important to act in alignment with your soul. Trust that courage will be available when you need it. This card could also be referring to the misuse of strength. Be aware of how your desires could be negatively affecting you and those around you.

···☆ 9. THE HERMIT ☆···

The Hermit shows up to call you back to yourself. If you've been giving too much of your energy away, it's time to fill your own cup. Find a way to acknowledge your physical and spiritual needs in deeply fulfilling ways. When you take time to fill your mind, body, and soul, you'll find that the path ahead has always been lit to guide you on your way. If the light of your path dims, then it's time to retreat within again. The Hermit is ruled by practical and patient Virgo. The earthy energy of Virgo understands the importance of going within. This could be as simple as making time to get more organized or take care of things you've been putting off. Be open to the wisdom of Virgo and the Hermit to clean up any distractions that could be dimming your path.

◁ ⌣ THE HERMIT REVERSED ⌣ ▷

The reversed expression of this card signals that you may be avoiding time alone with yourself. If you've been in a phase of constant distractions, are the distractions still serving your highest good? Alternatively, Hermit energy to an extreme can manifest as an overabundance of caution and an inability to be around others. If this resonates with you, ask yourself what small things you could do to walk forward and trust that your path will be lit.

⭐ 10. THE WHEEL OF FORTUNE ⭐

This potent card comes up as a reminder to find a point of stillness amid the constant changes life offers. The wheel of life, much like the cycles of the moon, is always moving. Even in our darkest moments, life must go on. This doesn't mean that we can't find peace or seek respite during the more turbulent phases. It does mean that our efforts to prevent difficult things from happening likely won't work. The Wheel of Fortune often indicates a time of great expansion, which could signal growth into a new phase or cycle of life. This card corresponds with the planet Jupiter, which signals a time of growth and possible good fortunes. If you've found yourself in a tumultuous time, this card can also appear as a reminder that nothing is permanent. An opportunity to excel may be just around the corner.

◁ THE WHEEL OF FORTUNE REVERSED ▷

When this card appears reversed, it can indicate that you're pushing against the natural flow of the Universe or are unwilling to accept changes. Trying to force a phase may backfire and will keep you from growing toward the best version of yourself. This card reversal may also indicate that your luck could be taking a turn for the worse. If this is the case, know that it's only temporary.

⋯☆ 11. JUSTICE ☆⋯

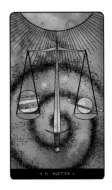

Justice can appear in your reading for a variety of reasons. The nature of this card is rooted in a deep need for truth. Truth is divine, and truth cannot exist without justice. Justice and equality are written into the fabric of our Universe and will always come to be eventually. This card could be showing up as a good omen in a legal situation, if you are in the right. If you are not in the right, this is your call to do what needs to be done to ensure that you're aligned with truth and the highest good for all. This card is ruled by the harmony-seeking sign of Libra. Libra will always strive to strike a perfect balance to please themselves and those around them. On a more personal level, this card may be an invitation to explore your balance, or lack of balance, in relationships with others. On the other hand, you may need to open yourself up more to receiving love and kindness from others. Be open to exploring where you can be in better balance with those you interact with.

◁⌣ JUSTICE REVERSED ⌣▷

This card's reversed expression calls you to assess where in your life you've been unjust or caused harm. If this is the case, take steps to clean up your side of the street and make impactful amends. This card reversed could also indicate an imbalance in your life. Be honest with yourself about areas that may be out of sync and what you can do to have more balance in your life.

···✩ 12. THE HANGED ONE ✩···

-★ 12 · THE HANGED ONE ★-

Receiving this card may indicate that it's time to sink into acceptance around a current situation. If you've found yourself pushing or fighting against something, this is your call to stop. The Hanged One calls you to try a different vantage point and be okay with doing nothing for a while. If you're stuck in a place of trying to force a situation, the answer can often be found in releasing and letting go of what you thought needed to be done. In your place of stillness, you may find that new ideas or the perfect answer come to you with little to no effort. This card is ruled by the planet Neptune, the king of the sea. The watery and intuitive energy associated with this card implies a need for spiritual connection. Trust that whatever you need will come with little to no force on your part.

◁◠ THE HANGED ONE REVERSED ◡▷

The reversed energy of this card suggests that you might be unwilling to let go of a situation. If you've been trying to force something to happen and there's no sign of it changing, this is a plea to let it go. Alternatively, this card's extreme reversed expression indicates that you've gone too far out into a dreamworld and are out of touch with reality.

⋯☆ 13. DEATH ☆⋯

This transformational card comes into your life to tell you it's time to let go of control. The Death card doesn't indicate a sudden loss, rather a slow and conscious evolution. This card is an energy of choosing to transform. What parts of yourself and your life are ready to disintegrate back into the earth to be molded into something new? This card is ruled by the sign of Scorpio. Scorpio energy is not afraid of the shadowy depths of the soul. In fact, that's where it feels most at peace. In what areas of your life are old ways of being and thinking holding you back? It's not only possible but likely that a better and more aligned version of yourself is waiting on the other side of the transformation. It's okay to release the parts of yourself that no longer serve you.

◄⌣ DEATH REVERSED ⌣►

The reversed expression of this card indicates that you're unwilling to let parts of yourself or your identity fall away to make room for new growth. The death process, in all its forms, can be daunting and scary. If this card has appeared reversed, it's calling you to address your fears around personal transformation so that you can continue to grow. Take small steps to envision what your life might look like if you choose to release undesirable parts of yourself or your life.

⋯✦ 14. TEMPERANCE ✦⋯

The energy of the Temperance card is soft but direct. Temperance calls you to have clear direction guided by your higher self but rooted in reality. The balance that Temperance calls for is tricky because it goes against our natural inclinations. Temperance doesn't ask you to spend every waking moment of your life deep in meditation. The energy of this card also doesn't want you to become absorbed by the pleasures of life. Temperance asks you to strike a balance between worlds. With one foot in the water and one on the earth, Temperance reminds you to be in flow while simultaneously rooted. The quest for spiritual truth can feel all-consuming at times. Truth-seeking Sagittarius is associated with this card. The energy of Sagittarius doesn't like fluff and calls you to get to the heart of every matter, again seeking balance between the spiritual world and the physical world.

◁〜 TEMPERANCE REVERSED 〜▷

When this card appears reversed, it often indicates that you're out of balance with spirit or earth. You may be in a cycle of chasing one adventure after another, avoiding your true calling. Or, on the other hand, you may be totally enthralled by your spiritual practice and have lost sight of the world around you. This reversed card calls you to find the moderation you need to move forward in a way that serves you and your community.

⭐ 15. THE DEVIL ⭐

The Devil asks you to approach your deepest desires and darkest fears head-on so you can integrate them. Without facing and integrating all parts of yourself, you'll never be whole, which will hinder your growth and happiness. Do you have any deep-seated beliefs that have kept you in a place of fear? This card calls you to face anything within you that you've feared or avoided. Facing these parts of yourself will feel difficult, but you'll soon find that full integration is the seat of your power. When you understand your fears, you can begin to work with them rather than against them. When you understand your addictive behaviors, you can begin to get to their root to move past them. This card aligns with earthy Capricorn, which could also signal a need for physical pleasures. Approach the energy of this card with a deep respect for the power of integrating light and darkness.

THE DEVIL REVERSED

The reversed energy of this card may show up if you've let your carnal desires run rampant. The physical sign of Capricorn savors all things physical. If your desires have begun to take over, it's time to rein them in and assess why you feel called to them. You'll better serve yourself and others when you're not being consumed by addictive behaviors. Alternatively, this reversed card could indicate that you're in denial about some aspects of yourself or your life.

⋯✦ 16. THE TOWER ✦⋯

The sudden and powerful strike of the Tower appears when it's time to break down the parts of your life that need to go. Tower moments can come into your life in a variety of ways. You may experience a sudden loss of a job, only to bring you to a job that's better suited for you. You may endure a sudden loss of a relationship, only to show you that you deserve much better. Alternatively, the experience of a Tower moment could be to help you learn about having a healthy sense of detachment from the physical world. The planet associated with this card is Mars, indicating that whatever change is on the precipice will be swift. The energy of this card can work within our minds as well, causing a sudden shift in our perspective around a situation. Mental awakenings can be just as painful as physical ones. Allow yourself to feel and process your emotions as they come up if the Tower card's energy manifests in your life.

◁◡ THE TOWER REVERSED ◡▷

This card's reversed expression indicates that you might be avoiding your feelings if you experienced a difficult situation or sudden awakening. It will be important for your growth to face what happened. If this feels too difficult, it's okay to ask for help. When you're able to process sudden changes and traumatic experiences, you'll be able to help others facing the same challenges. Healing is cyclical.

⋯☆ 17. THE STAR ☆⋯

The bright light of the Star comes in after the intensity of the Tower. This card appears to offer hope and inspiration. It's safe to believe that you are here for a purpose. The divine guidance and hope of the Star is not something outside of you but rather a force that dwells deep within. This is an energy you can turn to anytime you need to be inspired and renewed. The Star is ruled by the sign of Aquarius. Aquarius energy loves to stand out, is a freethinker, and believes in the good of others. This card's Aquarian energy calls you to believe in yourself and present yourself in the world as authentically as possible. Anytime you lose sight of your path, go within to connect with the divine wisdom of your inner light.

◁◡ THE DEVIL REVERSED ◡▷

When the Star shows up reversed, it may indicate that you're having difficulty seeing a way through. You may be experiencing a time of lost hope and believe that your life is doomed to failure. If you've faced many hardships, it can feel extremely vulnerable to have hope. Having hope means you might fail. However, if you never allow yourself to envision a brighter future, you'll never know the path to get there. This card reversed calls you to face your vulnerability around hoping for better and to find ways to see the good around you.

⋯✭ 18. THE MOON ✭⋯

The Moon card beckons you inward and asks you to explore your internal shadows. Shadow work is the act of making a conscious effort to explore your fears and repressed emotions; it's through performing this work that you become whole. The Moon card is your reminder to honor all facets of yourself. Be cautiously curious of new people or influences that come into your life and take time to get clear on their motives. It will be important for you to connect within before making any decisions. This card may also be calling you to connect to the energy of the moon. The moon has long been associated with the Divine Feminine, intuition, cycles, and the passage of time. Deep inner work requires a certain passivity and softness often associated with femininity. Be gentle with yourself as you embark on any shadow work.

◁⌣ THE MOON REVERSED ⌣▷

The reversed Moon card signifies a possible unveiling of confusion that may be on the horizon. Disorientating situations will begin to make more sense or clear up. People around you may open up about situations that once escaped you. Another aspect of the reversed Moon could indicate that fear, anxiety, or confusion has taken hold of you. The reversed Moon calls you close to reveal any stuck emotions that have become habit energy in your inner world. Lastly, if you've neglected your intuitive gifts, the reversed Moon may be asking you to explore them.

⭑ 19. THE SUN ⭑

The Sun card is always a welcome sight. This card calls you to play and enjoy the bounty of life around you. Call to mind the areas of your life that inspire the most joy and allow yourself to stay there for a moment. If you never allow yourself time to celebrate the happiest moments of life, they'll slip through your fingers, as all time does. Sometimes it's important to create your own joy in life. If you've gone through a difficult time or are in the midst of one now, how can you bring a little light from the sun into your life? Cultivate a childlike curiosity when it comes to embracing happiness. The Sun card also signals an abundance of health and vibrancy. It may be arriving to signal you to take action and enjoy this extra burst of energy.

THE SUN REVERSED

The reversed expression of this card indicates that you're cutting yourself off from experiencing joy. Have you caught yourself in a cycle of always seeing the glass half empty? This card is asking you to observe whether or not your denial of happiness is serving you. This card could also indicate a need to get in touch with your inner child. Perhaps there's part of your youth that needs some healing, or you just need to find more ways to invite play into your life.

⋯✫ 20. JUDGMENT ✫⋯

This incredibly understated and powerful card suggests an opportunity for two paths. The truth is, they both lead to the same place, although one may take longer. Awakenings and enlightenment come in all different forms throughout our lives. Some awakenings are brought on by deeply understanding how we've caused harm in the past, while others are brought on by deeply examining ourselves. Whichever path you choose, know that it will lead you on a journey of self-discovery to meet your higher self. This card shows up to indicate that a personal awakening is on the horizon. The planet associated with the Judgment card is Pluto. Pluto corresponds with both death and spirituality, promising a grand transformation. One might associate the energy of this card with answering a call directly from the Divine. It's time to take the call and meet a new version of yourself.

◁‿ JUDGMENT REVERSED ‿▷

This card's reversed expression indicates that you're avoiding an inner calling to wake up or make a big change. The life-changing transformations that the Judgment card suggests can certainly seem scary. If you've felt an inclination to face new ideas that you've been putting off, this card is a clear call to entertain the idea of a higher calling. What might a new and revolutionary path look like and feel like for you? The Universe is trying to connect with you.

⸳⸱✫ 21. THE WORLD ✫⸱⸳

Your long journey is coming to an end. As you walk through one phase into the next, it's time to honor and celebrate how far you've come and how much you've integrated. Though your expansion will never end, you've come to an important moment of culmination. The World card rolls into your life to honor and celebrate a time of fulfillment in your journey. You will likely attain a goal you've been working toward, either externally or internally. All four elements are associated with this card to represent your mastery and offer you safe passage as you move through to a new journey. The World is governed by the planet Saturn, the wise ruler of the sky that honors structure and discipline. The message of Saturn's energy is clear: As long as you're a physical being, you'll be ruled by the elements.

◁◡ THE WORLD REVERSED ◡▷

When the reversed World appears, it indicates that the closure you're seeking may be withheld at the moment. This withholding could be internal or external in source. It will be important for you to assess and determine the source of the pause in your journey. Maybe you're intentionally sabotaging your growth for fear of success, or you have a belief that you don't deserve to be rewarded. This reversed card could also indicate a need to fine-tune something on your path, as you're not quite ready to come to the end of this journey.

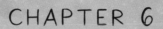

CHAPTER 6

THE MINOR ARCANA

Welcome to the vast world of the Minor Arcana. The number of cards in this section can seem overwhelming. However, when you break them down into their suits and understand some basic correspondences, you'll love and understand them in no time!

Think of the Major Arcana as the macro and the Minor Arcana as the micro areas of life. These cards speak to your day-to-day interactions. The Minor Arcana are still significant, but they're zoomed-in versions of the themes within the Major Arcana. Each suit speaks directly to different areas of our lives. For example, Pentacles associate with the physical world, Swords with the mind, Wands with action, and Cups with emotions.

Just like the Major Arcana, you'll see stories unfold within each of the four suits in the Minor Arcana. Because these cards revolve around day-to-day themes, the stories of the Minor Arcana are more personal, and will vary from person to person. Be open to the lessons each suit has to share with you and know that the lessons will evolve as you evolve.

···☆ THE CUPS ☆···

The Suit of Cups corresponds with the water element and deals with emotions. When cups show up in your readings, it's often a call to check in with your emotional world. Are there emotions that you're holding back, or, alternatively, are there emotions that are running your life? The Cups are an invitation to explore how your emotions are flowing or stuck within you and in your relationships.

The Cups also deal with the intuition, subconscious, and your ability to tune into the psychic realm. The subconscious is often hidden from us, shielding us from situations perhaps too difficult to process. The Cups give you glimpses into the world of your subconscious to help uncover areas you may be ready to explore. Allow your intuition to guide you when these nudges come up. Let your intuition and emotions flow like water to uncover anything prepared to surface.

⋯☆ ACE OF CUPS ☆⋯

Open yourself up to love. Your cup is or will be overflowing with loving and creative opportunities. Will you accept? This initiation into the suit of cups is a welcome invitation to revel in creativity and loving emotions both from the physical and the spirit world. If a new lover, friendship, or creative opportunity presents itself, this card is your sign to explore these opportunities. You won't be disappointed. The element of water associated with cups represents the energy of creativity and creation. This card could be indicative of a new child or birthing a new project into the world. The creative waters of the Universe are calling you to create in a way that feels good to you but also in a way that enables you to share and give to the world. Allow yourself to feel good and enjoy the creation of life.

◁◡ ACE OF CUPS REVERSED ◡▷

It may feel like the love and creativity in your life has been turned off and that the well has temporarily dried up. Perhaps you've been giving too much to those around you and need to find the love within yourself again before you can share with the world. A lack of emotions, love, and creative drive may have you feeling disconnected from Spirit. Everything is a phase, and so is this moment. Begin your journey back to Spirit by small acts of self-love daily.

···☆ TWO OF CUPS ☆···

Divine coupling is a gift not to be squandered. If you feel pulled to another in your life, whether it be a lover, friend, coconspirator, or creative partner, honor the opportunity. Treasure your sacred relationships like a precious gift because they are just that. This card is asking you to reflect on the divine nature of your relationships. Pause and drink in the magic it took to bring you and your most beloved partners into your life. This is a good time to assess whether your partnerships are expressing equal amounts of giving and taking. Equal reciprocity is the foundation of loving relationships. When you examine the most sacred relationships in your life, do you see opportunities where you can give more or be more receptive to receiving? Alternatively, if you're feeling a strong pull toward a new partnership, honor this message as an opportunity to explore.

◄‿ TWO OF CUPS REVERSED ‿►

All relationships travel through difficult phases, and you may be in one now. Every rough patch has a lesson. Even if it's too hard to see it at this moment, it will become clear eventually. If you are experiencing discord in a loving relationship, this is a call to approach it with love. Can this relationship be salvaged, or is it time to release it with love? Perhaps this is something you're unaware of, so be open to actively listening to those you're in a relationship with. You may have a lesson to learn.

⋯☆ THREE OF CUPS ☆⋯

This is an active, social, and celebratory card. The energy of this card can help you break through creative blocks. Perhaps it's time to collaborate with another, or perhaps it's time to draw inspiration from a different source. Seek to find the magic all around you in different ways and opportunities. At its core, this card is a call to celebrate in a way that feels good to you. If it's easy for you to find a reason to celebrate, run with it, and take some time to really drink it in. If you're able to come together with like-minded souls for a celebration, do so. This card is a call to be social! If you're having difficulty finding a reason to celebrate, start with the basics. What are the small things bringing you joy and comfort right now, and can you celebrate them? There's always something to celebrate.

◁⌣ THREE OF CUPS REVERSED ⌣▷

The opposite message of this card may indicate a time of sadness or depression. Perhaps you feel withdrawn from life in a way that it's nearly impossible to celebrate anything. Alternatively, when this card is expressed in excess, it could indicate that you're overindulging or taking your pleasure to an unhealthy extreme. You know where you fall here. Trust your instincts. If it's time to retreat from an excess of socializing and celebrating, take some time to rest and go within. If you're in a deep place where celebration seems impossible, it's always safe to ask for help.

···✫ FOUR OF CUPS ✫···

You may be in a place of confusion, feeling stuck, or simply unwilling to engage with life. It's okay to rest and take breaks. In fact, it's encouraged! However, when retreating from reality becomes the norm, it may be time to plug back into the fullness of life, even if it feels scary. If you've found yourself in a place of not wanting or caring to move forward, you may be cutting yourself off from experiences that would bring you true joy and happiness. Feeling the heights and depths of our emotions is a necessary part of the human experience. It's how we grow, learn, and become dynamic and fully integrated people. If your disconnection was caused by being hurt or left out, this is part of life too, but it won't last forever. Your cup will fill again, perhaps from an unexpected place. Try to find small ways to engage with life that feel safe and supportive to you and be open to unexpected gifts.

◄〜 FOUR OF CUPS REVERSED 〜►

In its reversed expression, the Four of Cups may be reflecting the opposite of apathy and indicate that you are very open to receiving insights from outside sources. You may find yourself in a place of being more sensitive and intuitive to outside hunches. Alternatively, it may be a call to actively retreat inward. The extreme of this card may be calling if you've been too open and receptive. It may be time to go into cocoon mode for a short period of time to restore and refresh.

⋯☆ FIVE OF CUPS ☆⋯

Emotional setbacks and upheavals are part of life. It's important to allow and feel all of your emotions. If you experienced a traumatic event and haven't allowed yourself to rage, cry, or be sad, it is time. You won't be able to move forward until you face the fullness of your loss. Feelings can feel permanent, but they aren't. They're a flowing river, always changing and renewing with fresh water. Even if it seems impossible, polar opposite emotions can coexist. You can hold deep loss in your heart, but also know that love, happiness, and success will be available to you again. Rather than focusing on only the negative, can you hold space for something that brings you joy, even if just for a moment? Trust that no matter the circumstances, there are brighter days ahead.

◂〰 FIVE OF CUPS REVERSED 〰▸

You may be feeling an extreme rush of mixed emotions. Allow it all to flow. The more you let yourself experience this intense wave of emotions, the faster you'll be able to integrate it into your life. This intensity will not last forever. Avoidance of your reality will not serve you here. You will have to face your fears at some point. The expression of this card reversed may also indicate that you've come to a place of acceptance and healing from past trauma or loss. You may have a renewed sense of peace after integrating a heavy experience that enabled you to learn and grow.

⸱⸱⸱✫ SIX OF CUPS ✫⸱⸱⸱

This card is bringing up a need to visit with the energies within you formed by your youth. Even if you think they're dormant, they rarely are. Much of our reality is dictated by the emotions and events we experienced at a young age. What information might your younger self share with you today? How have the emotions and experiences of your youth shaped you into the person you are now? If this version of you is something you've buried, it's time to approach your younger self with an inquisitive mind. The lessons of this card strive for harmony. Be open to healing old wounds within you or by a visitor from the past coming back into your life. This card also calls you to rejoice in happy memories and relationships from the past.

⸱◁⌣ SIX OF CUPS REVERSED ⌣▷⸱

You may be fixated on a past event that's keeping you from finding balance. It may be time to seek outside help to release these old wounds or traumas. If you find yourself clinging to happy memories because your present circumstances are difficult, try to find a balance between being present and having gratitude for the past. Alternatively, the polar opposite of this card may indicate that you're focusing only on the future and are spending too much time projecting (either positive or negative). Whatever the cause for your constant desire to escape the present moment, it is important to find ways to seek harmony.

⋯✦ SEVEN OF CUPS ✦⋯

Distractions abound, especially in this highly digital world. Have you found yourself in a place of overstimulation, rampant daydreaming, or too many choices? Tune in to your higher self and Spirit before committing to new endeavors. If you skip this precious step, you could fall prey to a deceptive opportunity. This card also echoes the importance of being grounded. With the overabundance of new opportunities and things this world can sometimes present us with, you may find value in connecting with nature. Spirit can be difficult to see and feel if you're in a constant state of flight. Find ways to plug into the present moment to gain a greater perspective on all of the choices around you. It's time to make a decision and move forward with total clarity and confidence.

◁⌣ SEVEN OF CUPS REVERSED ⌣▷

The reverse expression of this card may indicate a lack of choices. Perhaps you're feeling totally stuck with no ability to imagine something better for yourself. It will be important for you to open and expand your mind to new possibilities. On the other side of the spectrum, this card reversed might indicate that you're sailing through life with ease, checking in with your higher self often to make the choice you know is in the highest and best interest for you and those around you.

⋯☆ EIGHT OF CUPS ☆⋯

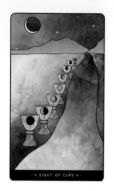

This card may be gently nudging you to release with love and put down a person or project that's no longer serving you. Deciding to release may not have anything to do with a failure on your part. It might just mean that a phase has ended, only to start a new one soon. Every time you walk away from something, it opens the door to new opportunities. If you're feeling a sense of loss or hurt around walking away from a situation or person, it's time to recognize that you've done all you can. It doesn't mean that the relationship or situation won't cycle back again, but now is the time to move to take care of yourself. Alternatively, if a situation has gone awry due to your choices, it's okay to let it go. Carrying guilt and shame won't serve you or anyone. Do what you can to clean up your side of the street, and then let it go.

◁⌣ EIGHT OF CUPS REVERSED ⌣▷

The reversed image of this card indicates a couple of possibilities. You may be finding yourself in a situation you know isn't good but are unwilling to leave. This reversed card is calling you to look at your situation with harsh clarity. It's also possible that you want to leave a situation when it's not time. Perhaps your current situation feels too daunting to face, and leaving seems easier. Take time to go within and assess the truth. Are you still needed? Is the phase really complete?

⋯☆ NINE OF CUPS ☆⋯

This card calls you to honor all of the good in your life right now. Perhaps you've been working toward emotional ease and contentment. This card indicates that you've arrived. What are some of the most rewarding and fulfilling experiences happening in your life right now? Can you take some time to sink into them and let them wash over you? Emotions are fleeting. It's so important to bask in our contentment when our cup is overflowing with pleasure and good feelings. So many of us are taught that we have to work hard to enjoy the finer things in life or that it's not safe to sink into pleasure. This card is calling you to abandon that kind of thinking and actively seek pleasurable moments and experiences. Sometimes being selfish is the self-care we need to best care for ourselves.

⊲〜 NINE OF CUPS REVERSED 〜⊳

Are you cutting yourself off from pleasure and gratitude? The opposing expression of this card could indicate that you may be rejecting the idea that you deserve to feel good about yourself. Try to find small ways to experience gratitude and satisfaction throughout your day. On the other hand, you may be feeling overwhelmed by things you thought would bring you happiness, only to realize it's an inside job. Can you find contentment within yourself, too?

⋯✮ TEN OF CUPS ✮⋯

You've formed deep and lasting relationships, the kinds that will endure a lifetime and beyond. The Ten of Cups calls you to reflect on the most sacred and important relationships you've formed. How have these sacred unions changed your life or shaped you into the person you are today? Alternatively, how have you shaped those around you who have an equal amount of reverence for you? Whether you've found these sorts of relationships within your blood family or a chosen family is irrelevant. Sacred bonds are formed in all kinds of relationships. Honor them all. This card indicates a time of completion but a desire for more. Be open to new ways to expand your most treasured relationships. There's no end to the joy sacred unions can bring you. Continue to allow your love to be reflected in one another.

◁⌣ TEN OF CUPS REVERSED ⌣▷

You may feel like harmony is eluding you. This card may come as a call to try to mend relationships that are important to you. Are there ways you can find more harmony in the relationships that are worth salvaging? On the other hand, the opposing energy of this card may indicate that you do live among harmonious relationships but are taking them for granted. Are there ways you can express your gratitude to those you love most?

⋯✰ PAGE OF CUPS ✰⋯

The Page of Cups invites you to approach intuitive information with curiosity. Perhaps working with your intuitive side is new or comes across as fanciful thinking. The energy of the Page is inquisitive in nature and calls you to be open to experiencing the intuitive realm from new perspectives. The energy of this card could also be drawing your attention to a new creative endeavor that you'll enjoy.

The youthful energy of the Page indicates that you might have more to learn in a certain area. The Page of Cups is often associated with someone with natural intuitive abilities. This card might be drawing your attention to a natural ability that you've been neglecting. If you've received nudges about exploring a new intuitive practice, the Page is your messenger to act on this calling.

◁⌣ PAGE OF CUPS REVERSED ⌣▷

The opposing expression of this card may indicate that you're ignoring intuitive messages or actively pushing them away. Alternatively, it's possible that you've gone to the other extreme and feel totally consumed by a dreamworld of your own making. Get clear about where you fall. If your intuitive abilities are knocking, but you feel unprepared, consider seeking outside help. If you've found yourself in a fantasy world, avoiding the real world, what are some small responsibilities you can take care of right now to help you feel more rooted in reality?

⋯☆ KNIGHT OF CUPS ☆⋯

The charming Knight has trotted in to rekindle the romance in your life. Be open to a renewed sense of romance and charm. If you're seeking a new romantic partner, one may be on the way. If you're in a committed relationship, how can you spark a new sense of passion for one another? If you're happily single, seek to inspire sensual encounters with yourself. Though the Knight may be the ideal partner, if that person isn't present, don't let it stop you from reveling in some romantic self-care. Because Knights are associated with more fiery qualities, the card may be a call to get outside of your comfort zone and try expressing yourself in more sensual and romantic ways. Do romance and sensuality make you feel uncomfortable? It's time to cozy up to the idea of trying something new. The Knight's desires can sometimes get in his way, so be aware of how your romantic inclinations affect you and those around you.

◁⌣ KNIGHT OF CUPS REVERSED ⌣▷

The reversed nature of the Knight of Cups can come off as overly seductive or even narcissistic. It's important to be honest about your desires in any relationship to avoid leading someone on, romantically or otherwise. This energy could also manifest as someone who's completely consumed by their desires to the detriment of others.

···☆ QUEEN OF CUPS ☆···

The Queen of Cups possesses double water energy, which makes her extremely sensitive, intuitive, and always in flow. Someone with the energy of the Queen is unfazed by nearly everything. Emotions and insights seem to flow through her like water and leave her completely unaffected. However, it's not that the Queen is unaffected by heavy emotions but has mastered the art of flowing with the ups and downs of them. This Queen is a deep feeler and someone whose presence alone will evoke healing. The Queen may be calling you to step even deeper into your intuitive abilities. She may also be asking you to feel your emotions more deeply, trusting that you'll be able to handle whatever arises.

◁◡ QUEEN OF CUPS REVERSED ◡▷

The reversed expression of this card can indicate that your intuitive abilities are out of control and that you might need better boundaries between you and Spirit. These boundaries may extend beyond Spirit and into the physical realm. The overly empathic queen can easily dip into the realm of people-pleasing to ease her sensitivities. It's important for you to place firm boundaries where needed to protect your gift of sensitivity. Lastly, the Queen's innate creative and intuitive abilities in excess could be used for nefarious purposes. If you've found yourself using your abilities for things not helping the highest and best of all, this is a call to reevaluate your motives.

⋯☆ KING OF CUPS ☆⋯

The calm King rests above the water as a master of his emotions. Truly nothing can faze him. The energy of the King understands when the actions of others are unworthy of his attention. He's able to maintain a calm and loving composure amid the chaos. The energy of this wise and loving leader calls you to be caring and diplomatic in all of your affairs. The King brings a layer of maturity that's needed in emotionally charged situations. If you find yourself in a situation, especially with those you love, that's emotionally challenging, this card is calling you to bring a balanced and compassionate level of communication to the conversation. You might be in a position where you don't want to take the high road. This card is suggesting that it's in your best interest to do just that.

◁◡ KING OF CUPS REVERSED ◡▷

The reversed manifestation of this card may show up as emotionally charged outbursts and anger. If you've not yet mastered your emotions, you might feel like you're being held captive by them and that they don't always come out in healthy ways. This energy can also present as extreme repression of your emotions, which will likely result in strong emotional outbursts. It's time to find more productive and loving ways to release your emotions for your sake and those around you.

⋯✮ THE PENTACLES ✮⋯

The Suit of Pentacles corresponds to the element of earth and deals with materiality, work, money, and physical comfort. When Pentacles show up in readings, it's a call to check in with realms pertaining to your body and the physical world. What is your relationship with work and money like? Do you feel nourished and supported? If you don't, what needs to change to feel better supported and held?

The Pentacles connect deeply with your ability to create within the material world. We each come into this world with gifts, and the Suit of Pentacles can help shed light on what those gifts are and how to bring them to fruition. This suit can also bring attention to financial disparities within yourself and the world and how to best heal them. We are spiritual beings in a physical world. Understanding and healing our relationship with the physical world is just as important as connecting to our spiritual nature.

⸱⸱⸱☆ ACE OF PENTACLES ☆⸱⸱⸱

The Ace of Pentacles is a welcome omen. It's your sign to move forward with any career or financial endeavors you've been thinking about. As with all ace cards, this card is a symbol of new beginnings and a fresh start. Because the Pentacles relate to the element of earth, it's a reminder that you are supported in your endeavors. Beyond financial support, this card calls you to feel the abundance all around you. If you've been stuck in a mentality of lack, try to look for things in your life that make you feel abundant and rich. Pentacles speak to materiality, so you may have an unexpected gift of material abundance coming your way. This card calls you to reflect on what true abundance means to you. When you have a clear understanding of what you need to feel safe, nurtured, and protected, you'll know how to move forward. Be open to different means of abundance.

◁⌣ ACE OF PENTACLES REVERSED ⌣▷

Just as this card can signal an unexpected windfall of abundance, the reversed message could mean the opposite. A sudden loss of material items, money, or beloved treasures could be on the horizon. If you experience a material loss, trust that it's for your highest good. On the other hand, if you've been stalling on starting a new project, career, or financial endeavor, this reversed message may be asking you to examine why that is. What do you need to feel more empowered in your ability to build a life you desire?

⭐ TWO OF PENTACLES ⭐

The Two of Pentacles asks you to examine the state of harmony in your work, goals, and self-care practice. You may be at a place in your life where harmony seems impossible. Trust that you're doing a perfect job of balancing the current situation. Whatever the case may be, this card wants to draw your attention to the symbiosis between different material aspects of your life. Your actions and inactions will affect all areas of your life. If it's a sense of busyness that's bringing you joy, savor it. If it's a sense of busyness that feels a little scary, trust in your ability to adapt and rise to the occasion. What feels like balance on the inside may not appear that way on the outside. You know what you need to be in a place of peace and harmony, even in a lively phase of life. Draw inspiration from nature to find harmony in your life.

◁ TWO OF PENTACLES REVERSED ▷

The Two of Pentacles reversed wants to bring your attention to a possible shift that could send waves of imbalance through your life. This could be something out of your control or something of your own doing. Be wary of taking on new projects, especially in your work life, that could cause discord in the long run. Get clear about how much you can really take on. Remember, no amount of money or material comfort is worth your peace of mind. Being in a state of imbalance for prolonged periods of time will always do more harm in the long run.

⸳⸳⸳☆ THREE OF PENTACLES ☆⸳⸳⸳

Growth toward the highest good for all will always require teamwork. In what areas of your work, material, and physical life can you glean wisdom from others? By building on the knowledge of many, strong foundations are formed. In the Two of Pentacles, you were busy and juggling many tasks. The arrival at the Three of Pentacles asks you to consider what your situation might look like if you asked for help, especially in areas that aren't your strong suit. Trust that your project will come together beautifully if everyone focuses on their personal talents. Be aware of ways that you could make a sacrifice to lift others in a current task at hand. Collaborative opportunities will often ask you to release some of your power, and that's okay. Celebrate the gifts everyone brings to the table, relish in your personal talents, and watch a new world flower before you.

◁⌣ THREE OF PENTACLES REVERSED ⌣▷

The Three of Pentacles reversed indicates that you need to examine how you're handling collaborative situations. This reversed message calls you to take an honest look at what you need to do to help the growth of all. Your personal choices, especially when it comes to group work, will affect others. Do you feel fulfilled with the work you're offering to the collective?

⋯☆ FOUR OF PENTACLES ☆⋯

This card speaks to you making financial progress in a way that supports your needs and comforts, or that perhaps you will be very soon. If it's taken you a long time to come to a place of comfort, don't forget to enjoy the fruits of your labor. As you continue to find comfort and meet your physical needs, the Four of Pentacles asks you to be aware of your relationship with money and physical comforts. Discipline is important, but it is also a balance. We all need and deserve physical care, but if we're not careful, our relationship with our creature comforts can lead to a sense of clinging and fear of loss. There's no amount of money that will leave you impervious to the elements of this life. Continue to be disciplined. There is power in your ability to focus and save resources, but don't let your ability to amass wealth become a false god.

◁◠ FOUR OF PENTACLES REVERSED ◡▷

When reversed, the Four of Pentacles sends a sharp message to assess your relationship with money and physical resources. It may indicate that you've taken your discipline to an extreme to the point of greed. Another perspective is the illusion of control or being out of control with your finances. When our finances seem totally out of control, it's common to turn to overspending. Overspending or overextending your resources offers a fleeting feeling of control, but it will always hurt you in the long run.

⭐ FIVE OF PENTACLES ⭐

You may be in or embarking on a patch of financial hardship. Like all things in life, honor and recognize that this too is a phase and that there is deep wisdom to gain from all situations. Regardless of how you may have come to a situation of physical loss, it's important to note that focusing on the cause of the loss will likely not fix the situation. By focusing on the lack, you will likely create more lack. There's nothing wrong with seeking help. However, if the help you're seeking has closed its doors to you, trust that what you need will come. Your solution may not materialize immediately, and that's okay. Continue to walk your path and have faith in your inner guidance. There are solutions to all problems, and it may be easier than you think. This is a time to lean on your internal strength.

◁ FIVE OF PENTACLES REVERSED ▷

This card reversed indicates an unwillingness to find your own solutions. You've likely found yourself in a state of being angry, defeatist, and stuck. Your anger is valid, but there's no need to carry it with you throughout this storm. Feel into your anger around financial and physical losses in your life and decide to move forward. The burden of anger will only weigh you down. Alternatively, this card reversed could mean a shift toward a financial improvement and that any blocks have been removed. Be honest with yourself in determining where this card lands for you.

⸱⸱⸱☆ SIX OF PENTACLES ☆⸱⸱⸱

Opening your heart to be in a place of receptivity requires a certain amount of trust. This card comes as a message that it's safe to receive. It also reminds you that it's important to give. Equitable community care is an ultimate act of love and is necessary for the well-being of all people. The Six of Pentacles asks you to be open to both giving and receiving. After the Five of Pentacles, you may be in a position of great need. If help comes, accept it with open arms. Giving and receiving goes both ways, and you'll never know how much the act of receiving a gift may benefit the giver as well. If you find yourself in a place of need, are there any resources being offered to you that you haven't made use of? Now is the time to open yourself up to receiving aid. If you find yourself in a place of abundance, where can your resources be used in the most equitable way?

⸱◁◡ SIX OF PENTACLES REVERSED ◡▷⸱

The Six of Pentacles reversed can indicate a couple of different scenarios. The reversed message of this card calls you to sit in any discomfort around giving in a meaningful way. Alternatively, this card reversed may be calling you to focus on how you're giving and receiving in relationship to yourself. Has self-care taken a back seat in your life? If it has, it's time to give to yourself and place self-care on your list of priorities.

⋯✦ SEVEN OF PENTACLES ✦⋯

It's time to pause, reflect, and allow your work to grow without interruption. You've made great strides toward your material goals, work, and physical growth. It may not be time to harvest yet, but it's safe to take a break to honor all that you've accomplished up to this point. Perfectionism is often a lie we tell ourselves to hold on to things too tightly. But, if you never pause for reflection, you might lose sight of your original purpose. This card also signals a time to reflect on how best to move forward. Perhaps you've reached a place in your work where you need to release one aspect to pick up something new. Alternatively, this card may be calling you to stick with your task at hand. Taking breaks to appreciate your work will translate to a more sustainable way of working toward your long-term goals.

◂〰 SEVEN OF PENTACLES REVERSED 〰▸

The reversed message of this card suggests that you likely do not feel at peace or excited about your work. Perhaps you've been striving hard with little result, or you're feeling scattered in the work you're doing. It may be time to abandon a project that's not working or seek out more meaningful work. Get clear about the kind of work that excites you and gives you a true sense of accomplishment. What changes can you make in your life to support a work situation that fulfills you?

⋯☆ EIGHT OF PENTACLES ☆⋯

If you find yourself to be a somewhat scattered person in your work, this card is a call to focus on and refine one skill. Alternatively, you may be called to learn a new craft, apprentice, or do a repetitive job in order to complete a task. There's value in each scenario. The mundane holds deep wisdom, as does your ability to master a set of skills. Seek to find the deeper teachings within the simplest of tasks. There is great satisfaction in the mastery of a new skill. Trust that your attention to detail and improvement of your capabilities will lead you to a satisfying and necessary space in your evolution and in the evolution of your community. The work ahead may seem daunting, but it will be worth it in the end. On your path toward mastery, you may discover that true satisfaction comes from the work rather than the end product. You have everything you need to accomplish the work in front of you.

⊲〜 EIGHT OF PENTACLES REVERSED 〜▷

The reversed message of this card indicates that you might be avoiding certain work or willfully doing a poor job. It's important to remember that your work affects those around you. It could also indicate that you find the work effortless, and therefore you've discredited its value. The Eight of Pentacles reversed calls you to seek work that you find more satisfying or to change your perspective and try to see the value in monotonous activities.

···✿ NINE OF PENTACLES ✿···

Luxuriate and enjoy your successes. Whether you have come into financial wealth, an abundance of physical comfort, or simply the satisfaction of a job well done, this card calls you to savor the moment. This abundance could have come to you through your own hard work or from an unexpected source. Regardless of the source, be sure to honor what brings you pleasure. This card calls you to savor your hard work and find a sense of pride and accomplishment. It's safe to pat yourself on the back and revel in your achievements. This card may also indicate that you'll find yourself in a space of financial freedom soon. Enjoy the direction in which your success leads.

◁◡ NINE OF PENTACLES REVERSED ◡▷

The reversed expression of this card offers the suggestion that you've lost focus on projects that you once hoped would bring you success. You may feel scattered or at a loss for how to get where you want to be. It could also mean that you're not letting yourself accept the successes in your life as real. Perhaps you've found yourself in a perpetual state of "waiting for the other shoe to drop." If you've found yourself in a place of perceived failure, know that success is still available to you. It's time to find small ways to act in alignment with your goals. If you've found yourself in a place of being unwilling to fully accept your successes, try to take small actions each day to honor the work you've accomplished.

⋯✬ TEN OF PENTACLES ✬⋯

The Ten of Pentacles reveals that you're on your way or have already arrived at a place of generational wealth. Remember, although "wealth" may mean gobs of money in your bank account, it may have other meanings as well. Perhaps you and your family are exceptionally healthy or have found yourselves living in a lush paradise with bountiful harvests from the land. Whatever this wealth indicates to you, the message of this card is that it is here to stay. This card offers a reminder not to take your abundance for granted and to share it with others. Don't lose sight of the magic of life and the power of giving. Beyond monetary well-being, the Ten of Pentacles also indicates a desire to find physical abundance in the mundane of life.

◁〜 TEN OF PENTACLES REVERSED 〜▷

Because this card speaks to family connections, the reversed meaning could indicate financial trouble within your immediate or extended family. On a more personal level, this expression of the card may be calling you to reflect on where your values lie. If you've found yourself consumed with amassing wealth, it's time to pause and reflect on whether that's bringing you true happiness. It is possible that you'll find more joy with fewer material items. Has your material status caused you to feel stifled in any way? If so, what changes can you make to find more freedom or abundance in different forms?

···☆ PAGE OF PENTACLES ☆···

Our earthy Page of Pentacles represents being in a place of hope, curiosity, and prospects of a new journey. It's okay to dream and imagine new possibilities and ways to be in the world. This is your invitation to take it all in and absorb the world around you with an inquisitive fascination. Perhaps it's time to start something new or begin the early stages of a new manifestation. The childlike wonder of the Page will give you new perspectives that have the potential to lead to successes that may seem impossible at the moment. Continue to stay on your path with an open and inquisitive mind. All of the Pages are open to learning new ways of approaching old ideas. This may be your call to begin a new task using an unusual or unheard-of method.

◁⌣ PAGE OF PENTACLES REVERSED ⌣▷

The reversed Page of Pentacles indicates that you may be being too rigid in your approach to a new project, which could be making you feel stuck or stagnant. This kind of approach could also lead to failure. Try to find ways to keep your inquisitive mind intact on new journeys. Alternatively, the Page of Pentacles reversed could mean that you're in a place of complete avoidance around new projects. It may be time to examine your relationship with work or school to see where you might be cutting yourself off from new growth.

···☆ KNIGHT OF PENTACLES ☆···

The Knight of Pentacles indicates that you're ready to do what needs to be done to complete a task at hand. Even if you can see your work ahead and find it daunting, you're ready to do what it takes. The fiery energy of all of the Knights can be seen as the final push you need to take action. In relation to the Suit of Pentacles, this will usually pertain to work, school, or material projects. The energy of the Knight is often expressed as very practical and conservative. This could present in your life as taking care of monotonous tasks knowing that the end result will land you where you need to be. It's a call for you to face any projects or tasks you've been putting off head-on. Know that when you do decide to face these challenges, you'll have everything you need to accomplish your goals.

◁◡ KNIGHT OF PENTACLES REVERSED ◡▷

This Knight of Pentacles reversed indicates you need to find a routine. You may find the act of completing daily tasks unbearable or forget them entirely. If there's something you want to accomplish that's been eluding you, you will need to implement more structure in your life. Alternatively, this card may show up more internally in a way that's causing you to stagnate. If you've taken your conservatism to an extreme level, it may be preventing you from growing or seeing other perspectives. Try to keep an open mind, especially when it comes to work projects or your finances.

⭐ QUEEN OF PENTACLES ⭐

The Queen of Pentacles is the embodiment of Mother Earth. This Queen is nurturing and in flow with the rhythms of nature. She carries the deep wisdom of mother energy. This card may appear in your life to commend you on your caring nature. It may also be asking you to find ways to tune in to the energy of Mother Earth and her innate wisdom. In relation to the Pentacles, this Queen speaks to your ability to care for your family in a deep way. The Queen calls you to go beyond merely offering material needs but to also offer comfort to those around you. The Queen of Pentacles is a lush jungle of wisdom and capable of balancing the needs of herself and others.

QUEEN OF PENTACLES REVERSED

The reversed energy of this card indicates that you may be out of touch with the natural world. When was the last time you went for a walk outside or gazed in awe at the beauty of nature? If you can't remember, it's time to plug into the natural world from which you came. When the Queen of Pentacles is overly expressive, it could present as people-pleasing and neglecting your self-care. Be aware of how your desire to care for others is manifesting in your life. If you've left yourself out, make your care a priority before you care for others.

⋯☆ KING OF PENTACLES ☆⋯

The King of Pentacles is secure and comfortable in his place of material wealth and power. The energy of this card speaks to someone with great leadership skills, especially around money and work. The King doesn't just accomplish his goals. He leads others to do the same. This King is able to see opportunities that others might not and act on them in a way that will always yield results. The position of power that the King of Pentacles has found himself in may leave him feeling slightly possessive over his fortress and material possessions. If you find yourself in a position of power and wealth, you may also feel yourself holding it quite tightly. The energy of this card calls you to move toward material desires with total confidence.

◁◡ KING OF PENTACLES REVERSED ◡▷

The reversed nature of this card can express as someone not living up to their full potential or experiencing a big loss financially or at work. If you're currently experiencing a financial loss or setback at work, trust that you'll be able to rise to your previous stature. It might just require a different strategy. When the energy of this card is amplified, it may show up as extreme stubbornness and greed. If you find yourself putting your desire to amass wealth in front of all other things in your life, it might be time to examine your relationship with money and material possessions.

⭐ THE SWORDS ⭐

The Suit of Swords corresponds with the air element and deals with the mind, communication, and ideas. When Swords show up in your readings, it's often a call to seek mental clarity and refine your communication. What is the quality of your thoughts like, confused and cluttered, or clear and concise? How is your communication with yourself and others? The Swords are an invitation to explore how your mind and communication might be holding you back or ready to have you speak up.

The Swords also deal with ideas and your ability to receive inspiration. When you're cut off from ideas and whispers from spirit, the mind can feel cluttered and confused. The Suit of Swords can help you cut through the confusion and take action based on divine inspiration. Calls of action from the Suit of Swords are often swift and can initially be painful. Trust that any call to grow in the realms of communication will serve the highest good of yourself and those around you.

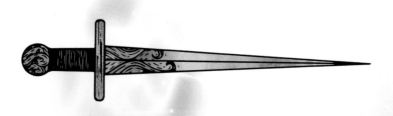

⋯☆ ACE OF SWORDS ☆⋯

The Ace of Swords is a clear call to action. Illusions cannot be present in the midst of this card. It is supreme truth and knowing. It asks you to be bold, open, and honest about who you are and what your beliefs are. It's not in your highest good to continue being or acting like someone you're not. If you've found yourself in situations where you haven't been totally honest or have been afraid to step on toes, you cannot hold back anymore. This card might also indicate a mental breakthrough. If you've been experiencing confusion around a certain topic or person, the answers are within you. Be open to receiving the clarity you need, and then act. The sword is in front of you, ready to grab. It's time to speak out in truth for the highest and best for yourself and those around you.

◁⌣ ACE OF SWORDS REVERSED ⌣▷

The reversed expression of this card indicates extreme confusion. It's also possible that you may be intentionally withholding the truth. The longer you stay in this place, the more it will hurt you in the end. Be honest with yourself. Alternatively, this card might represent that you've taken your desire to spread your truth too far and may be damaging others in the process. If your words of truth cause harm, that's worth gaining clarity about as well.

···☆ TWO OF SWORDS ☆···

Opposing thoughts and ideas are making it difficult for you to make a decision. It's time to get clear about the pros and cons of each side. Choosing what's right doesn't always mean doing what's easy. Sometimes the path you need to take might, initially, be more difficult. If you've weighed the pros and cons, trust that the path you take will eventually lead you and those around you to a better place. The crossing of the swords indicates that you may be intentionally shutting down in regard to a hard decision. You might even find yourself in a situation where you've shut people out of your life because you find it too difficult to face the truth. This card is calling you to restore balance by approaching decisions you've been neglecting with openness. Your internal struggles are an invitation for deep growth.

◁◡ TWO OF SWORDS REVERSED ◡▷

The reversed nature of this card may indicate that there's no good answer to your question at hand. It may be that no matter the choice you make, someone will be harmed. Alternatively, it could mean that there are forces out of your control, making it impossible for you to have a clear idea of what's really happening. If this is the case, you must rely on your intuition. However, if an internal struggle has you stuck, it might be time to seek outside help.

⸱⸱⸱☆ THREE OF SWORDS ☆⸱⸱⸱

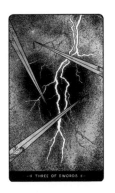

Emotional pain is part of life. What matters most is how we walk through it when it occurs. Do you have emotional wounds that are fresh or freshly reopened? In what ways can you honor your pain, maybe even bring it to light, so it can be faced and healed? The sting of grief may lessen over time, but you will continue to be re-wounded if you're unwilling to face your pain. This card is a call for deep self-compassion and care. Your sorrow may be from others or from within. If you tend to speak negatively about yourself, it's time to get to the root of why you're inflicting so much pain on yourself so you can heal. If an emotional wound came from the outside, it's time to heal. Deep work like this may require help from someone else, and that's okay. Your healing is of utmost importance.

◁〜 THREE OF SWORDS REVERSED 〜▷

The energy of this card reversed indicates an emotional wound that's been completely blocked, that you're unwilling to face. Your pain may be manifesting in unexpected and harmful ways toward yourself and others. It's also possible that you've intentionally chosen to hold on to your pain because of the attention it brings. It's time to ask yourself whether being a martyr really serves your highest good.

⋯☆ FOUR OF SWORDS ☆⋯

The Four of Swords is a strong call to retreat within. The work of the mind and truth is not easy and will require rest. If you recently faced a storm of emotional turbulence, it may be over, but your healing work is not. Part of healing includes deep rest and reflection. In such a busy world, you might feel like this is an unnecessary step, but this couldn't be further from the truth. Your precious mind needs time to integrate to come back stronger and wiser.

Have confidence that your progress will not be lost. All of the work you've been doing is right where you left it and will be there, ready for you to pick up again. Remember that you are not responsible for the rate of your healing. Trust that there are larger forces at play here. The rest you need is the rest you need. This is not a time to set rigid deadlines.

◁⌣ FOUR OF SWORDS REVERSED ⌣▷

The reversed energy of this card may indicate that you've been in a place of rest and that it's time to come out of your cave. Perhaps you've been putting off returning to work, friends, dating, or family, and this is your call to begin putting yourself out there again. Alternatively, this card reversed could be expressed as internal distress from going within. If this is the case, try to relax into the moment without forcing an outcome.

···☆ FIVE OF SWORDS ☆···

You may find yourself in a victorious situation, but at what cost? If the cost of being right has caused you to harm yourself or others, is it worth it? Part of our human nature is a desire to be right. Can you find the lessons in this deep need to be right? This card indicates that it might be in your best interest to take the high road. Is it possible to be right without picking a fight? Fives indicate a tumultuous situation, and it is best to proceed with caution and clarity. If you were recently defeated, is there anything to be learned from the situation? Your lesson could be as simple as letting go of your need to be right. Will holding on to a loss, even if you were right, help you in the end? It might be time to apologize or make amends for harm caused in the name of being right. If you need to release yourself from your actions to move forward, what might an apology to yourself look like?

·◁◡ FIVE OF SWORDS REVERSED ◡▷·

The reversed energy of this card suggests that you might be stuck reliving a fight or argument and unable to let it go. If you are, is it truly serving you to rehash it? What do you need to find closure around a difficult feud, even if the other person is unwilling to admit fault? Alternatively, if you were victorious but can now see the error in your ways, how can you make amends?

⸱⸱⸱☆ SIX OF SWORDS ☆⸱⸱⸱

You are embarking on an important journey. Even if the path ahead seems rocky, know that it's in your best interest and will land you in a lighter mental place. Keep an open mind. This path toward smoother times may not be a physical journey. Might your mind be trying to take you to a higher place, to blend past and present into one for greater unity and understanding? If you're facing a tumultuous situation, internal journeys can be quiet but profound. How can you move beyond the limits of your mind to find a greater perspective? Once you reach your destination, you may find it's time to release the old mental baggage you've been holding on to for far too long. This journey seeks to clarify and unify.

◁⌣ SIX OF SWORDS REVERSED ⌣▷

The reversal of this card indicates that you might be refusing to change, move on, or see a situation from a higher perspective. It's time to examine what's causing you to remain in such a tumultuous situation. You may be fearful of your ability to grow into new ways of being and thinking. Growth can be just as scary as staying in a harmful situation, but it won't serve you in the long run.

···☆ SEVEN OF SWORDS ☆···

If you're planning to make a move or change, this card comes as a call to be extremely careful and strategic in your planning. Alternatively, if you're engaged in something that you know is deceitful, this card may be an indication to examine your motives and assess whether it's worth it, even if you do get away with it. The airy qualities of the Swords sometimes give us spontaneous ideas, but that doesn't mean they're all worth acting on. Sometimes, our ideas require careful planning before executing. Alternatively, this card could indicate that you are indeed acting in the highest and best interests of yourself and others. Even though some may see your actions as dishonest, if you know something needs to be done, your actions are necessary. Regardless of the nature of your planned actions, taking the necessary time to plan is imperative.

◁◡ SEVEN OF SWORDS REVERSED ◡▷

The reversed expression of this card indicates that you may have acted in haste in a recent situation. Perhaps you were caught in a deceitful act and are now paying the consequences. If so, it's time to own up and be honest with yourself and those around you. On the other hand, this reversed card may indicate a need to be cautious of deceitful plotting against you. Get clear about the motives of those closest to you.

⋯☆ EIGHT OF SWORDS ☆⋯

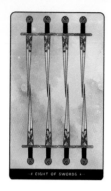

As a suit rooted in the intellect, this card indicates that any bondage you're experiencing results from within your mind. Though all of us can face external limitations and blocks, it's not uncommon that the firmest and most damaging limits are ones we place on ourselves. How has your limited thinking caused you to shrink, and is it serving anyone? The self-imposed prison walls in your mind are not only hurting you but also affect the expansion of others. When you break free from self-doubt, you will inspire others to do the same. What would you be doing or saying in your life right now if you weren't afraid to fail? This isn't to say failure won't happen if you step out of your comfort zone—it undoubtedly will—but you'll learn and grow when it does.

◁〰 EIGHT OF SWORDS REVERSED 〰▷

This rare positive reversed card indicates that you are freeing or have freed yourself from limiting beliefs. You may feel a great sense of release in your ability to express yourself authentically. Alternatively, when we look at the reversal as an amplification of its meaning, it could indicate that you're experiencing a deluge of harsh inner criticism. If this is the case, you may benefit from seeking outside counsel.

⋯☆ NINE OF SWORDS ☆⋯

The Nine of Swords might feel like a stormy cloud following you around. You might be experiencing thoughts and fears that seem insurmountable in their heaviness. This card calls you to ask whether all the fears you're experiencing are real. Or, have some of them been expanded and amplified by your magical mind? Anxiety and worry often immobilize us, but when we make room for acceptance, we can find the strength to move forward, even in difficult times. It is okay to experience fear and worry, but will continuing to ruminate make the result any less painful? Where can you find love and compassion for yourself in situations that are out of your control? Don't forget to use the tools you have available to you to better cope with difficult matters of the mind.

◁⌣ NINE OF SWORDS REVERSED ⌣▷

When this card shows up reversed, it may indicate that your fears have completely immobilized you. You may find yourself in a position of deep shame, despair, or guilt and feel unwilling to approach these deep-seated feelings. If a way through your fear seems impossible, it's always safe to seek outside help. Alternatively, the reversed expression of this card may indicate a loosening of your anxiety.

···✪ TEN OF SWORDS ✪···

Tens always indicate an end of a cycle, and this ending is very pronounced. This completion of a cycle may be within you or outside of you, but it will likely regard matters of truth, justice, and authenticity. Perhaps you've experienced a sudden awakening, causing you to act more authentically. Alternatively, there may be a harmful situation that's finally coming to an end. The sudden shock may not be as bad as you initially think. Some endings are painful, and some are worthy of celebration. Either way, an end of a cycle always indicates the promise of a new phase. If you've experienced deep wounds, it is safe to look ahead and plan for the future. It's okay to tend to your wounds, but don't get stuck there. It's time to move on and open yourself up to brighter days ahead.

◄ ⌣ TEN OF SWORDS REVERSED ⌣ ►

When this card shows up reversed, it may indicate that you're unwilling to move forward. You might be stuck in the past and in denial about a change you need to make, even if it's harming you or others. Even the image suggests a clinging. The swords, upside down, should fall but remain lodged in the ground. This message is calling you to face where you might be clinging to ideas not serving your evolution.

⭐ PAGE OF SWORDS ⭐

You may be experiencing an influx of new ideas, thoughts, and inspirations. Exciting as some of them may be, your job is to sit and experience all that is coming at you, not to act. Sometimes when exciting opportunities come along, it might tempt you to run off in a specific direction before gaining all of the necessary information. The curious nature of the Page of Swords calls you to stay and continue learning with an open mind before acting. When it comes to disagreements and sharing thoughts, you might feel encouraged to approach them in new ways. This Page suggests that a certain level of detached curiosity could come in handy in conversation. This kind of approach will certainly aid you in some situations but may not prove beneficial in the long run. It's up to you to know when it is time to step into a more active role.

◁～ PAGE OF SWORDS REVERSED ～▷

If your curiosity and new ideas have gotten the better of you, this card may appear reversed. An overflow of new thoughts and ideas could land you in a place of feeling stuck rather than excited. Additionally, this card could indicate that you've actively cut yourself off from learning new things and expanding your mind. You might find yourself in a place of rigidness that keeps you from growing.

···☆ KNIGHT OF SWORDS ☆···

The brave energy of the Knight understands when it's time to act, and act they do. This card indicates that you're in a space of walking, definitely and head-on, into a storm, regardless of the outcome. When a perfect opportunity presents itself at just the right moment, you'll know in your heart when it's time to act. The Knight of Swords heeds this call and moves ahead at full force. There are times when bold assertiveness is quite necessary. If this is a trait that doesn't come naturally to you, trust you'll have the strength when you need it. There's often a downside to impulsive acts. It's important to be willing to face the consequences of your actions, even if you're in the right. Though the Knight is guided by passion, it is also guided by truth. Even with steep consequences, you may find your actions justifiable in the end.

·◁⌣ KNIGHT OF SWORDS REVERSED ⌣▷·

The energy of the Knight is extremely active. In its reversed expression, it may present as either overactive to an unhealthy extent or total inaction. When this Knight is overactive, it can indicate that you may be pushing yourself into a place of burnout and exhaustion. At the other extreme is being far too lax about injustices, resulting in harm by lack of action.

⋯☆ QUEEN OF SWORDS ☆⋯

The Queen of Swords indicates someone who's seen their share of sorrows but is wiser and stronger due to their life path. This Queen exerts a sense of confidence and sureness that may come off as abrasive to some. If you identify with this sentiment, don't let others sway you in your firmness. Boundaries are sacred acts of self-care, even when they may offend others. The arrival of this Queen is calling you to rise to an intimidating situation with confidence. Trust that everything you've learned will give you the words you need. It's time for you to set boundaries in any situation where people have been taking advantage of you. The boldness of your self-preservation will grant you deep mental peace.

◁◡ QUEEN OF SWORDS REVERSED ◡▷

When this Queen appears reversed, the energy often presents as quite demanding and angry. Martyrdom is also a common theme of the reversed expression of this card. You may believe that you've paid your dues, and because of this, you refuse to learn, grow, or do anything that may impact you negatively, even at the expense of others. This card calls you to reflect on how your emotions may be clouding your judgments and actions toward others.

⋯☆ KING OF SWORDS ☆⋯

This King is a master of his mind. His words are always precise and can lovingly cut through to the heart of any matter. The King of Swords is not someone you want to get into a verbal battle with, as you'll surely lose. This card shows up to say that perfect clarity and wise words are available to you. Be open to the possibility that you can master your mind and thoughts. The King is able to make his point with little effort because he knows his words are rooted in wisdom. The King's confidence can be felt when he speaks and calls you to find your confidence as well. If you're embarking on a situation where you need to speak out, call on the confident energy of this King to guide you. The power of speech rooted in truth has the ability to change the hearts and minds of many. Don't doubt your capabilities.

◁◠ KING OF SWORDS REVERSED ◡▷

This King reversed will often come across as power-hungry and manipulative. This King has a strong and clear voice that can be used for positive change or corruption. If you're in a position of power, this card may be calling you to get clear about how you're using your voice. Alternatively, the reversed energy of this card could be expressed as a total lack of communication. Even if you're in a place of power, you may find yourself totally speechless and unwilling to take a stand. This card is a wake-up call to find the clarity you need to speak up.

···☆ THE WANDS ☆···

The Suit of Wands corresponds with the element of fire and deals with action, energy, and passion. When wands show up in your readings, it's often a call to notice how you're using your energy and assess where you need to take action or stop withhold action. How is working towards your goals going smoothly, or do your actions feel forced? The Wands can help shed light on your next steps to get you where you want to go.

The Suit of Wands also deals with passion and power. A lack of passion in your life might cause your actions to feel robotic or like nothing really matters. The fiery energy of the Wands wants to help you uncover where your true passions lie, so you feel empowered to be of better service to yourself and those around you. Alternatively, suppose you are allowing others to drain you. In that case, the Suit of Wands can help you determine how to better use and conserve your energy for optimal results. Don't be afraid of your passions and your ability to alchemize new worlds!

⭐ ACE OF WANDS ⭐

A new creation is ready to be born. The Ace cards always indicate new beginnings. The fiery energy of the Wands suit likely means you're feeling the intense stirring of something that not only wants but also needs to come to life. Like a snake ready to strike, you might be feeling an intense need to take action. The wait is over. It's time to act. If you're presented with a new project, creative endeavor, or opportunity, this is your sign to grab it and run. The Suit of Wands indicates an abundance of energy. You can move forward with confidence that you'll have all of the energy and strength you need to accomplish the task at hand. You are supported by the energy of the radiant sun!

ACE OF WANDS REVERSED

The pure and intense energy of the Ace of Wands reversed can come as quite a shock. This card, in its reversed expression, may indicate a new project blowing up in front of you. If you're in the midst of a project that you feel like you're losing control of, this is a call to refocus your energy with more control. Alternatively, this card reversed might mean a total lack of desire and energy, even with new prospects. If this is the case, it might be time to shift gears and seek something that you find truly inspiring.

···☆ TWO OF WANDS ☆···

You are standing at a powerful threshold, and it may be time to make a decision. It's important to decide where you intend to invest your energy before moving forward. Without careful planning, your energy may be squandered. This card is a call to plan for options you're presented with before making a move. This will help you make the best use of your energy. This card also indicates that your choices may have a long-lasting effect on your life and those around you. Be open to new ways of working and consider investigating new pathways before taking action. The road ahead may be long. It's important to consider that your inner resources aren't infinite. You'll need to be open to a variety of options to reach your goal.

◁◡ TWO OF WANDS REVERSED ◡▷

The reversed energy of this card indicates that you may be rushing into things too quickly. Your actions will likely have long-lasting consequences, and it might be time to retreat and regroup before moving forward. Alternatively, this card may express that you're confused about where to go with your life and feel completely unsure. If this is the case, it is time to go within for quiet reflection before planning or taking action.

···☆ THREE OF WANDS ☆···

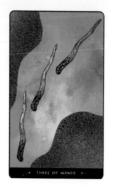

The Three of Wands suggests a time of activity and growth in a project or desire. The wheels are in motion, decisions have been made, and you've planned accordingly. It's time for you to watch as your plans unfold. As your actions continue, be open to calling in others to aid you. It's likely you'll need help as your plans continue to unfold. If you're in a position of growth, this card may be calling you to keep a close eye on your plans as they unfold.

Your plans are at an early stage and can still go in a variety of directions. It will be important for you to remain grounded as you watch your work unfold in front of you. Similar to the Two of Wands, this card reminds you to use your energy wisely.

◁⌣ THREE OF WANDS REVERSED ⌣▷

The reversed Three of Wands indicates that a recent endeavor may have failed. You put yourself and work out into the world but have come back empty-handed. This is part of life and part of expressing your desires. Learn from your mistakes, rest up, and commit to moving forward. On the other hand, this card reversed may indicate that you're holding back and could go further if you'd trust yourself.

⋯☆ FOUR OF WANDS ☆⋯

It is time to celebrate! This card indicates a time of great joy and festivities. Fours offer stability and structure, which you've undoubtedly built in some area of your life. This card could also indicate welcome support from others. You may feel yourself pulled to your chosen family for additional stability. If this is the case, this card is your call to honor your desires. Because this card symbolizes structure, it may indicate the culmination of something that will bring you a sense of stability or an important milestone. Be open to receiving the fruits of your labor. Take time to honor where you've created solid foundations in your life. If you never take the time to honor your progress, you'll likely lose momentum. You deserve to celebrate your efforts.

◄◡ FOUR OF WANDS REVERSED ◡►

The reversed energy of this card can still indicate joy and celebration, just in a different way. You may be called to seek joy within or to find ways to celebrate what you already have in your life. Happiness does not need to originate from outward successes. On the other hand, this card could also indicate a snag in your plan before fulfillment or that you've lost a sense of stability.

⋯☆ FIVE OF WANDS ☆⋯

When working with others toward a long-sought goal, it's not uncommon to run into conflicts. When it comes to passion projects, energies will likely run high. This card is an important reminder to hear other people out. Just because you believe you're right doesn't mean there aren't other paths to the same goal. Be open to learning from others, especially in regard to topics you're passionate about. This card could also indicate a need to rise to a challenge to continue your growth. Expanding your desires often includes growing pains. It may be time to push yourself into an uncomfortable environment to advance your development to the next level. Are there uncomfortable situations or conversations you've been avoiding? It's time to face them with optimism.

◂⌣ FIVE OF WANDS REVERSED ⌣▸

When this card is reversed, it may indicate that a competition won't turn out in your favor or that you'll experience an unexpected attack. If you're caught off guard, take this as a small setback but don't let it stop you from moving forward. This reversed card could also mean that when disagreements do arise, you may be unwilling to hear others out. A quarrel of this nature would result in no one making progress. Your ability to be open to other viewpoints will help you in the long run.

···✫ SIX OF WANDS ✫···

This card suggests that a triumph is on the horizon. On your way to victory, it will be important to keep your eye on the prize and continue to believe in yourself. If you don't feel like you're worthy of success or are facing some sort of imposter syndrome, your ability to succeed may become clouded. You'll still have work to do. Continue on your path ahead with confidence. This is a cooperative card. Accept help from others when offered and reach out when you know you're out of your area of expertise. A refusal to acknowledge when you need help could hold you back. Celebrate small successes along the way. Act as though you've already succeeded while keeping a vigilant eye on your end goal.

◁⌣ SIX OF WANDS REVERSED ⌣▷

The energy of this card reversed indicates that you may be overconfident in your ability to succeed without putting in the necessary effort. If you're working toward a goal, take an honest look at where you may need to optimize your efforts or return to the planning phase. Is it possible that you're letting your ego lead more than it should? Alternatively, this card reversed could mean a public setback ahead of you.

⋯☆ SEVEN OF WANDS ☆⋯

Similar to the Six of Wands, this card also implies success, but not in the same way. You may be faced with an intense situation or conflict over your progress. Trust in your ability to continue on even against adversity. You may find that there are others vying for a similar position or end goal. Stand your ground and continue to focus on your path forward. This card also calls you to be cautious of how you expend your energy. It may be that you're worried or anxious about something that's not actually happening or that your fears are completely out of your control. If you know there's nothing that can be done about what or who is trying to pull you from your path, don't waste your energy.

◄⌣ SEVEN OF WANDS REVERSED ⌣►

The reversed expression of this card indicates that you may be feeling unsure about your current path. Maybe you've begun questioning yourself and your actions. It will be important for you to find ways to gain your confidence back to move forward and find success. On the other hand, you may be in a position of feeling attacked by others, or even yourself. Have you put too much on your plate, or do you have people coming at you from all directions making demands? If this is the case, it's time to stand up for yourself.

⋯☆ EIGHT OF WANDS ☆⋯

This active but simple card has more to say than meets the eye. You may be at the precipice of a quick change or be required to make a rapid decision. The active and fiery energy of Wands may lead you to make hasty decisions. Even though things may seem to be moving quickly, be sure to gain clarity before your next move. You've come a long way on a journey, but all things come to an end. This card may also indicate that a long journey may be ending soon. What loose ends do you have to tie up? Are there any final changes you feel called to tend to before ending a big project? This card could indicate a need to ground yourself before moving forward. If you've found yourself in a constant state of doing, how can you tend to any personal needs before jumping back into action?

◂◝ EIGHT OF WANDS REVERSED ◜▸

The reversed energy of this card could indicate that you're intentionally dragging something out, even if you know it is, in fact, in your best interest to walk away. Get clear about why you may be holding on too tightly to a project or person. Can you try to see the possible benefits of allowing a natural conclusion? Alternatively, you may find yourself in a situation where you need to step up and be more forceful and decisive in your need to make a change.

⋯☆ NINE OF WANDS ☆⋯

Every journey you embark upon will lend a variety of experiences, both positive and negative. You may find yourself in a victorious position, but not without some losses. Your losses could be mental, physical, or both. Wherever you are in your process, take time to tend to your wounds. Trust that your mixed bag of experiences will lead you to higher ground, even if you find yourself in a moment of pain. Alternatively, this card could indicate that due to previous hardships, you're spending too much time and energy guarding yourself. This card may be calling you to be more aware of how you're using your energy and whether it's serving you (or not serving you). Honor your feelings and tend to your wounds, but don't allow your hardships to rule over you.

◁⌣ NINE OF WANDS REVERSED ⌣▷

When this card appears reversed, it could indicate that you're coming up against a conflict that you're not prepared for or that has caught you off guard. If this is the case, it may be time to retreat rather than risk an unnecessary failure. This card reversed could also mean you're experiencing anxiety around a situation without real cause. It's time to question the deep roots of any unfounded anxiety that's coming up.

⋯☆ TEN OF WANDS ☆⋯

The intense energy of Wands sometimes entices us to take on more than we can handle. If you've found yourself in a situation where you have more than you can or want to do, this card is a call to be honest about your workload. Even if you've found yourself at the end of a project, you may feel like the weight of it is too much to bear. Has coming into a new status or position opened doors to new problems? Alternatively, this card may indicate that you've been holding on too tightly to something, even though you know it's time to let go. This card is your call to assess what needs to go and what truly needs to stay. It's time to call all of your energy back.

◁◡ TEN OF WANDS REVERSED ◡▷

The reversed expression of this card indicates that you might be well aware that you have too much on your plate but that you're unwilling to let go of anything. If you've found yourself in a position of choosing to do too much, this card is calling you to be honest about why that may be. Are you afraid that no one else will be able to do quite as good a job? Or, is your overworking a source of self-sabotage? Perhaps you've been brought up with the belief that you have to overwork to be successful. What would your life look like if you believed you could be successful without overworking?

···✰ PAGE OF WANDS ✰···

The Page of Wands sits in awe at all the possible roads before them. The energy of this card often indicates excitement and creativity. Perhaps you're the type of person who's always looking ahead to the next thing and ready to run at every opportunity. If you don't identify with this energy, how can you inspire this spark within yourself? Whether you believe it or not, there are always messages and new pathways ready for you to embark on. Can you find ways to tune in to Spirit for guidance? Can you partake in activities that make you feel inspired and alive? It's within this sense of feeling truly alive and creative that new ideas come to us. The Page of Wands calls you to be open and willing to feel the joy and warmth life has to offer.

◁〜 PAGE OF WANDS REVERSED 〜▷

When this card shows up reversed, it may indicate a couple of things. You may be in a phase of extreme adventure on the verge of being reckless. Is it possible that your need to experience new things is having negative consequences on you and those you love most? Alternatively, this card could indicate that you're running into problems with a new project.

⋯☆ KNIGHT OF WANDS ☆⋯

The double fire energy of the Knight of Wands indicates an intense amount of momentum. This card may indicate that you're experiencing an exceptionally intense moment in your life. You will likely feel a push so strong that you'll have to take action. This intense moment could be seen as a welcome gift or a burden. The choice is yours. If you're in the middle of a passion-filled time in your life, enjoy it while it's here. Fires often burn hot but fast. Like all things, this too will be a phase, but this phase could be particularly short-lived. The intensity associated with this card could cause you to act in ways you'll regret in the future. Even though your energy may be high, don't forget to check in with your higher self from time to time before rushing into things.

◁◡ KNIGHT OF WANDS REVERSED ◡▷

The reversed expression of this card may indicate that you're using your energy unwisely. Be aware and cautious about where you're spending all of your time and energy. Is what you're focused on at the moment in the highest good for you and those around you? In what areas of your life might it serve you to conserve your energy or change directions? Alternatively, this card reversed could indicate a total lack of energy.

···☆ QUEEN OF WANDS ☆···

The Queen of Wands indicates a focused and easeful use of energy, where you're able to bend every outcome to your desires. This kind of precision requires practice and extreme confidence in your abilities, but this Queen makes it look easy to the untrained eye. The energy of this card may show up as someone who's working against larger forces. The Queen calls you to be strategic and wise about every step you take. Trust that your fire of energy will not burn out if you maintain a sense of calm focus with every action you take. It's likely that many look up to you. How can you best be of service in this role as a wise and radiant leader? Let your creativity and desire for positive change shine until others have no choice but to see you.

◄╰ QUEEN OF WANDS REVERSED ╮►

The reversed nature of this card indicates that you may have trouble trusting your natural abilities. You may be stuck in a place of low self-confidence. If you've found yourself in a well of doubt, what small actions can you begin to take to build your confidence again? Alternatively, if your confidence has become overactive, it may be time to assess whether your boldness has turned into prideful boasting or rudeness.

⋯☆ KING OF WANDS ☆⋯

This charming King often presents as someone in a leadership position. This King has mastered the art of balancing action and planning. The King understands how to use his energy in the most efficient way. This card reflects an inner knowing that periods of action must be balanced by periods of inaction and planning. The King is compassionate but also understands the necessity for taking actions that are sometimes difficult. This card indicates that you have no problem delegating roles when necessary. If this doesn't speak to you, it may be time to assess where you need to be open to appointing others to assist you in your vision. Real change requires a commanding leader with both a bold vision and a big heart.

◁〜 KING OF WANDS REVERSED 〜▷

When this card appears reversed, it often indicates someone in power who's taking advantage of their leadership role. If you find yourself in a leadership role and are letting your sense of power get in the way of what is right, it's time to assess how your actions may be harming others. A leader's role requires serving not only themselves but the masses as well. On the other hand, this card reversed may indicate a total lack of power or an unwillingness to lead. Be open to your strengths and how they could serve the world.

KEY PHRASES

0. The Fool
Curiosity, childlike wonder, ready for an adventure

1. The Magician
Initiation, using your resources, infinite power

2. The High Priestess
Intuition, sacred knowledge, the subconscious

3. The Empress
Fertility, physical senses, regard for Mother Nature

4. The Emperor
Power, leadership, force

5. The Hierophant
Ancestral knowledge, guidance, new teacher

6. The Lovers
Harmony, new relationships, important decisions

7. The Chariot
Clear direction, in flow, swift changes

8. Strength
Courage, lust, desire to share your light

9. The Hermit
Self-reflection, patience, filling your cup

10. The Wheel of Fortune
Phases, luck, finding stillness amid the changes

11. Justice
Divine balance, truth, equality

12. The Hanged One
A shift in perspective, surrendering to what is, open to alternative insights

13. Death
Needed change, transformations, release

14. Temperance
Moderation, a balance between earth and spirit, direction

15. The Devil
Power, integrating the shadow self, addictive habits

16. The Tower
Flash of insight, sudden disruption, a moment of chaos

17. The Star
Rebirth, guiding light, inspiration from within

18. The Moon
Illusions, concealed information, intuitive connection

19. The Sun
Play, savoring happiness, health

20. Judgment
Grand awakening, answering an inner calling, reincarnation

21. The World
End of a cycle, integration, culmination

◊ Ace of Cups
New loving relationships, creation, in flow with the universe

◊ Two of Cups
Divine coupling, equal reciprocity, respecting relationships

◊ Three of Cups
Celebrate life, collaborate to create, dance with your emotions

◊ Four of Cups
Meditation, open to outside wisdom, feeling stuck

◊ Five of Cups
Emotional loss, setbacks, holding space for despair and hope

◊ Six of Cups
Childhood memories, harmony with others, healing old wounds

◊ Seven of Cups
An abundance of choices, visioning new opportunities, inner clarity

◊ Eight of Cups
Releasing with love, moving on, end of a cycle

◊ Nine of Cups
Gratitude, allowing pleasure, basking in good feelings

◊ Ten of Cups
Sacred relationships, long-term unions, family harmony

◊ Page of Cups
Intuitive abilities, open to learning, new insights

◊ Knight of Cups
Romantic encounters, charm, fiery relationships

◊ Queen of Cups
Highly intuitive, in flow with emotions, empathetic

◊ King of Cups
Master of emotions, caring, contemplative

◊ Ace of Pentacles
New beginnings, new job opportunities, new streams of abundance

◊ Two of Pentacles
Finding balance, peace amidst the storm, flexibility

◊ Three of Pentacles
Working together, personal artistry, symbiotic growth

◊ **Four of Pentacles**
Financial control, amassing wealth, discipline

◊ **Five of Pentacles**
Financial hardship, scarcity mind-set, inner strength

◊ **Six of Pentacles**
Equitable offerings, sustainable growth, giving and receiving

◊ **Seven of Pentacles**
Reflection, trusting the process, allowing growth

◊ **Eight of Pentacles**
Mastery of skills, building a solid foundation, peace in the mundane

◊ **Nine of Pentacles**
Honor your successes, allow pleasure, self-reliance

◊ **Ten of Pentacles**
Generational wealth, long-term success, seeing abundance in the everyday

◊ **Page of Pentacles**
New pathways, curiosity, learning new techniques

◊ **Knight of Pentacles**
Steady work, doing what needs to be done, conservatism

◊ **Queen of Pentacles**
Nurturing heart, balanced caretaker, in sync with Mother Nature

◊ **King of Pentacles**
Master at manifesting, solid leader, material success

◊ **Ace of Swords**
Clarity, mental breakthroughs, a need to speak truth

◊ **Two of Swords**
Choices, weighing all options, opposing ideas

◊ **Three of Swords**
Emotional wounds, self-compassion, grief healing

◊ **Four of Swords**
Going within, needed rest, allowing healing

◊ **Five of Swords**
Need to be right, painful loss or victory, learning a lesson

◊ **Six of Swords**
Moving beyond obstacles, gaining new perspective, releasing mental baggage

◊ **Seven of Swords**
Careful planning, strategic actions, finding an unusual solution

◊ **Eight of Swords**
Negative self-talk, self-imposed imprisonment, approaching perceived limitations

◊ **Nine of Swords**
Acceptance, moving through fear, allowing your feelings

◊ **Ten of Swords**
Sudden ending, painful awakening, moving on

◊ **Page of Swords**
Taking in new ideas, open to new forms of communication, waiting to act

◊ **Knight of Swords**
Swift action, defending truth, determined and decisive

◊ **Queen of Swords**
Healthy boundaries, direct but loving communication, self-preservation

◊ **King of Swords**
Confidence, clarity of mind, clear and commanding communication

◊ **Ace of Wands**
Fiery beginnings, passion, potential

◊ **Two of Wands**
Focused energy, important choices, planning for the future

◊ **Three of Wands**
Moving ahead, cautious optimism, business partnerships

◊ **Four of Wands**
Celebrate success, milestones, pause for gratitude

◊ **Five of Wands**
Growth, competition, learning from others

◊ **Six of Wands**
Successful endeavors, believing in yourself, cooperative leadership

◊ **Seven of Wands**
Protecting your growth, courage while facing adversity, continuing on

◊ **Eight of Wands**
Quick action, sudden change or end, need to ground

◊ **Nine of Wands**
Victory at any cost, tending to wounds, fear of being hurt

◊ **Ten of Wands**
Overburdened, calling your power back, new responsibilities

◊ **Page of Wands**
Creative, open to new journeys, zest for life

◊ **Knight of Wands**
Emboldened action, passion, impulsiveness

◊ **Queen of Wands**
Focused energy, confidence, master at manifesting

◊ **King of Wands**
Commanding presence, natural leader, ability to delegate

MESSAGE FROM THE AUTHOR

When the world falls apart around you, you embark on a new career path, or you're unsure in which direction to go, the tarot will remind you of the course you want to take. The tarot whispers to your higher self to continue to grow into the best version of yourself.

If you feel drawn to the tarot, take the call. It has a message for you. Let it be a window into your soul and a wise and honest companion. When you open yourself up to its layered wisdom, you can't help but expand.

Allow the growth, allow the sorrow, and allow the joy. It's all part of your journey.

Love, light, and shadow,
Cassie

THANK YOU

Endless gratitude to those who made this book series possible! Thank you to all of the sweet souls at Quarto Publishing, especially my editor, Keyla. Thank you to my designer, Sydney, who's been a creative force for Zenned Out since its inception many years ago. Sincere gratitude to my infinitely patient husband, who, unwaveringly and lovingly, supports every new journey I embark upon. Eternal gratitude to my guides on the other side, including my sweet grandmother and father.

Thank you to every single one of my fans, followers, and supporters. I see you, and I love you. You light me up every day and give me the energy to continue sharing my gifts.

Love 🤍 Light

Cassie

···✯ ABOUT THE AUTHOR ✯···

Cassie Uhl is an artist, author, gentle guide to spirit, and lead goddess of her business, Zenned Out. She created Zenned Out with the mission to build a brand that normalizes spirituality. Her goal is to offer accessible information to enable you to understand a variety of spiritual practices and put them into action!

Inspired by her open-minded grandmother, Cassie has been meditating and working with her energy since her teenage years. Though she's always been inspired by nature, she began working more intuitively and magickally with nature in 2016 after losing her native British-born grandmother. Losing her grandmother spurred Cassie to reclaim her spiritual heritage, engross herself in the seasonal cycles, and begin walking the path of ancient British shamanism.

Through Zenned Out, Cassie has self-published her best-selling *Goddess Discovery Book* and oracle card deck, *The Ritual Deck*. In 2020, she authored *The Zenned Out Guide to Understanding Auras*, *The Zenned Out Guide to Understanding Chakras*, *The Zenned Out Guide to Understanding Crystals*, and *The Zenned Out Guide to Understanding The Wheel of the Year*. Learn more about Cassie and her other products at **ZennedOut.com** and visit her blog **ZennedOut.com/blog** for an abundance of free resources!

·•◊ REFERENCES ◊•·

Buchanan, Michelle. *Numerology: Discover Your Future, Life Purpose and Destiny from Your Birth Date and Name*. Carlsbad, CA: Hay House, 2015.

Esselmont, Brigit. *The Ultimate Guide to Tarot Card Meanings*. CreateSpace, 2019.

Kynes, Sandra. *Llewellyn's Complete Book of Correspondences: A Comprehensive & Cross-Referenced Resource for Pagans & Wiccans*. Woodbury, MN: Llewellyn Publications, 2013.

Louis, Anthony. *Complete Book of Tarot: A Comprehensive Guide*. Woodbury, MN: Llewellyn Publications, 2016.

Place, Robert M. *The Tarot: History, Symbolism, and Divination*. New York: Penguin Group, 2005.

Pollack, Rachel. *Seventy-Eight Degrees of Wisdom: A Tarot Journey to Self-Awareness*. Newburyport, MA: Red Wheel/Weiser, 2019.

Porter, Tracy. *Tarot Companion: An Essential Reference Guide*. St. Paul, MN: Llewellyn Publications, 2000.

Zalewski, Pat, and Chris Zalewski. *The Magical Tarot of the Golden Dawn: Divination, Meditation and High Magical Teachings*. London: Aeon Books, 2008.

Put your new knowledge of the Tarot into practice with *The Zenned Out Journey Tarot* deck and guidebook.

AVAILABLE NOW